Top Tips for Raising a Golden Retriever Right

Socialize. Introduce your Golden puppy to lots of people, places, sights and sounds. A puppy needs to learn about the world beyond his own backyard if he is to mature into a stable, well-behaved adult. Continue his socialization through his first year. The broader his experience, the more golden he will be.

Teach. Your Golden did not come already programmed or pre-trained. You have to teach him correct behavior and good manners just like you did (or will do) with your kids.

The Golden Ps: Praise, Patience and Practice. Use all three to train your Golden. Goldens learn best when trained with praise, patience and lots of practice (which equals attention—"Yippee!"—in a dog's eye view). In return he will give you a fourth "P," a Positive(-ly wonderful!) attitude in everything he does.

Exercise. Keep your Golden healthy, happy and content with a generous dose of daily exercise.

Remember your dog is an athlete who needs to run, play, swim and do busy, active things. Also remember, a tired and satisfied dog won't channel his energy into destructive entertainment.

Dental hygiene. Clean your Golden's teeth—he will live longer! Weekly tooth brushing is one of your most important Golden chores.

Lean cuisines. Feed a quality dog food and do not add table scraps or supplements. Obesity is a health hazard and just 10 extra pounds can shorten your dog's life.

Emergency action. Become an Emergency Expert so you can recognize and handle canine accidents and emergencies.

Spay and neuter. Have your companion Golden spayed or neutered at the earliest possible age.

External Features of the Golden Retriever

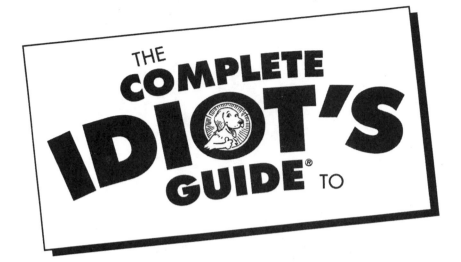

THE
COMPLETE
IDIOT'S
GUIDE® TO

Golden Retrievers

by Nona Kilgore Bauer

Howell Book House   Alpha Books
Divisions of Macmillan General Reference USA
A Pearson Education Macmillan Company
1633 Broadway, New York, NY 10019-6785

Macmillan Publishing books may be purchased for business or sales promotional use. For information please write: Special Markets Department, Macmillan Publishing USA, 1633 Broadway, New York, NY 10019-6785.

International Standard Book Number: 1-58245-033-1
Library of Congress Catalog Card Number: 98-49290

01 00 99   8 7 6 5 4 3 2 1

Interpretation of the printing code: the rightmost number of the first series of numbers is the year of the book's printing; the rightmost number of the second series of numbers is the number of the book's printing. For example, a printing code of 99-1 shows that the first printing occurred in 1999.

Printed in the United States of America

Alpha Development Team

Publisher
Kathy Nebenhaus

Editorial Director
Gary M. Krebs

Managing Editor
Bob Shuman

Marketing Brand Manager
Felice Primeau

Acquisitions Editor
Jessica Faust

Assistant Editor
Georgette Blau

Development Editors
Phil Kitchel
Amy Zavatto

Production Team

Editor
Amanda Pisani

Production Editor
Mark Enochs

Cover Designer
Mike Freeland

Illustrator
Bryan Hendrix

Photography
Winter Churchill Photography
Dennis Gray

Designer
George McKeon

Indexer
Riofrancos & Co. Indexes

Layout/Proofreading
Sean Monkhouse/Angel Perez

Contents at a Glance

Contents

Foreword

Why wasn't Nona Bauer writing a book for idiots when we bought our first Golden Retriever? I know it was meant for us, but unfortunately it didn't exist.

We did almost everything incorrectly when we bought our first dog. We bought him through a newspaper advertisement. We had no crate and not a clue about housetraining. We did not have a fenced yard or any outside enclosure. We had no dog toys. We had no veterinarian. We knew nothing about canine nutrition. Grooming for good health was totally foreign to us. Training was a complete unknown. Looking back on that time, I wonder how in the blazes we convinced anyone to sell us a puppy. But, we did! And, with high hopes and great pride, we drove home with our prized puppy in my arms.

Max was proof of the resiliency and adaptability of this incredible breed. He came to live with two well-intentioned but foolish new owners. We were young and enthusiastic. He was younger and even more enthusiastic. Wild times, wild behavior, and hysteria resulted from this meeting of puppy and owners.

Had we but known . . .

Given a choice, we inevitably made the wrong one each time. For example, let's look at the word, "Come." This appeared to us as a rather simple concept and one we could teach our fine new friend quickly and easily. I sat in one corner of the kitchen and held him. In the other corner of the room, Dave stood and called his name and used the word "come." Oh, how joyfully Max raced to Dave. Dave swept him up in his arms, planted kisses on his fuzzy muzzle and pronounced him brilliant. I agreed completely. After doing this exercise in our kitchen rather regularly for a few days, we just knew he knew the meaning of the word. One afternoon, Max and I were in our unfenced yard when he spotted a rabbit. He immediately dropped what he had been doing and gave chase through a field of clover. I assumed this was a good time to use the word "come." Picture it: He is heading due north. I call his name and holler, "Come." He keeps heading due north. A bit more loudly and insistently, I yell, "Max, come!" He keeps heading due north. I scream his name and screech the word "come" at the top of my lungs. He keeps right on heading due north.

Here, then, are the lessons we learned that afternoon: Max learned that he only had to come when he felt like coming. I learned that Max only had to come when he felt like coming. (The rabbit learned to keep heading due north!) How grand it would have been for both of us and for Max if we could have checked through Nona's book for advice on training a dog.

Had we but known . . .

Prior to owning Max, I had no idea what "grooming" meant. Frankly, it sounded fairly "frou frou" to me. Imagine my shock and surprise when we learned that this grooming business must be done regularly for a dog's health, not to mention his handsome beauty. Well, now, if it was for his health, we were all for it. So, of course, we raced out and bought scissors, clippers, combs, brushes, shampoo, conditioner, etc. A day of grooming was not Max's idea of fun. And frankly, after all the years of chasing him down for his bath, of innumerable wrestling matches over nail trimming, of the countless battles about trimming that hair between his ticklish toes, it wasn't our idea of fun either. In fact each grooming session resembled war games—games which he generally won. How lovely it might have been for Max and for us if we could have checked through Nona's book for advice on grooming a dog.

Had we but known . . .

Max enjoyed almost anything and everything, but he truly *loved* whatever was new. He simply had an enormous sense of curiosity burning within him. Once on a visit hundreds of miles from home when he was almost 14, Dave and I took Max for a walk through the neighborhood. As we strolled by one house, a small young dog leaped off his porch and barked at all of us. Max ignored him. The youngster wouldn't stop. He kept barking and leaping, leaping and barking. Finally, Max strolled closer to the porch to get a better look at him. Simultaneously, the homeowner opened the front door to call her dog inside. In a surprise show of agility and speed, Max catapulted himself over the young dog and raced into the house. Touring quickly through their living and dining rooms, Max stopped for a long back roll in the master bedroom. Sheepishly, Dave and I apologized to the laughing homeowner. Once again, the lure of investigating something new had captured Max's imagination. And again, I wonder at how we might have used this aspect of his temperament for training if we could have checked through Nona's book.

Over the years I have questioned how much greater a dog he would have become had we known what we were doing. In spite of our ignorance, Max was a magnificent Golden Retriever. He was a blend of beauty and brains, physical and mental soundness, nobility and humor, and dignity and silliness. We would have changed nothing about this good friend and companion. Yet, the very fact of our lack of knowledge haunts me always. Might he have enjoyed life even more had we known more, had we known all of the material contained in this wonderful book?

Joyce Kinghorn, Past President, Golden Retriever Club of America

Introduction

Before you set off on your Golden Print Adventure, let me draw you a dog map, sort of an idiot's guide to the *Idiot's Guide!* This book is divided into five parts, each one devoted to a different element of your dog's life or your own dog responsibilities (every Golden person has them). Parts 1 and 2 cover the Golden Retriever as a breed and how to find a stable, healthy pup. Parts 3 and 4 discuss training, behavior, and health care, the foundation of your golden life. Part 5 will tell you all the fun stuff about Golden Retriever activities and senior dog care, and I'll include some fundamental information "bytes" about living a happy and successful golden life together.

I should warn you in advance: you might find that I occasionally repeat myself, because certain dog facts and rules are important enough to bear repetition, and I will lose sleep if you don't remember them. If you notice it, that's great because it means you remember what I said the first time. Good dog!

As you travel through this book, you'll find the following little "road signs," tip boxes with snippets of information that range from important to just plain funny dog facts.

Bet You Didn't Know

These boxes are just what they're named, either serious or humorous dog details that could improve your golden life—yours and your dog's!

Doggy Do's

These tip boxes offer hints and reminders about handling various canine situations. Do not overlook the "Do's."

When To Call The Vet

These boxes supplement your Golden's health care. They contain new information or reinforce important facts. Vet-wise owners have healthier Goldens!

Doggy Don'ts

These are the opposite of Do's and equally important. These boxes warn you about doggy hazards in canine care and behavior that you might be unaware of or might overlook. Be sure you check them out!

Acknowledgments

Writing dog books requires an incredible amount of energy and stick-with-it-ness, which is tough if you're also a dog owner, breeder, trainer, and professional dog hugger like myself. It's also hard on a dog writer's family: my very patient husband and five children who graciously allowed me extra time and space so I could work, and my beloved Goldens who waited anxiously for our farm runs every day!

No dog author is truly "original." We are all rather a composite of dedicated dog breeders, trainers, veterinarians, scientists, behaviorists—writers all—who have passed along their experience, knowledge, and expertise to improve the life of dogs and their people. From Great Dane to Dandy Dinmont fanciers, all dog people are truly golden when it comes to sharing, and I am indebted to those many experts who through the years have helped shape my life with dogs.

A special thank you to Dr. Kaye Fuller, Texas veterinarian, trainer, and long-time breeder of KC Golden Retrievers, who reviewed the health information in this book. She's one more example of a golden human being. Many thanks to the staff at Alpha who helped fine-tune this manuscript, Mark Enochs, production editor and Anne Owen, copy editor.

And a huge Hurrah for Amanda Pisani, my editor and personal cheering section of one—how I needed her patience and support!

One final thank you: to the 20-plus Goldens, both here and at the Rainbow Bridge, who have shared my life over the past 30 years and to every pup I've ever bred. You inspired me to dog delights beyond my imagination, and you filled my days with love, joy, and dreams. What more could I ask of life?

About the Author

Nona Kilgore Bauer is a confessed Golden Retriever junkie. She's been a Golden nut for over 30 years, and there's no hope on her horizon for a cure (not that she wants one!). Nona is totally addicted to this almost-human canine and into overkill on Golden Retriever paraphernalia. Her closet is full of T-shirts and sweat shirts with grinning Golden faces on their fronts, and she doesn't freak out when she finds silky you-know-what in her salad bowl. Because her dogs sleep with her, her king-size bed was purchased so the dogs would have more room. (But you already guessed that!) Nona might be an idiot about her Goldens, but she wouldn't have it any other way.

Nona and her husband live on what some folks refer to as Retriever Heaven. Their 150-acre farm is dedicated to the training, welfare, and happiness of the dogs that live there and the ones that visit to train or just have fun. With a four-acre lake a few giant Golden strides from their back door, their dogs swim and play water games every day from spring to fall. Aside from their regular training sessions and Nona's writing time, their retrievers spend their days waiting, just waiting, for their daily walks and grand outdoor adventures. On the Bauer farm, every day is filled with Gold.

Nona and her dogs are blessed with dog friends from all walks of life: breeders, veterinarians, professional trainers, and accomplished amateurs who, along with the dogs, have been the inspiration behind her pen (well, nowadays it's her computer). She is a member of the Golden Retriever Club of America, the Golden Retriever Club of St. Louis and their rescue committee, the Mississippi Valley Retriever Club, the Quincy Kennel Club, and writes a weekly newspaper column on general pet care.

She has judged field trials, hunt tests, and working tests with some of the best retriever folks in the Midwest and believes that she has learned valuable lessons from each of them. Nona has trained several of her Goldens to Master Hunter level, two to qualified All-Age status in the field, and many more to obedience and other working titles.

Nona's Goldens are part of her public speaking life as well, and together they travel to schools, clubs, and writers' conferences to acquaint the non-dog world about the joys of living with and training dogs.

During the past 10 years, three of her Goldens have "worked" as nursing home therapists, coaxing smiles and tears from old folks who seldom laugh or cry. Each monthly visit proves the power of a friendly paw and velvet muzzle on the knee. No wonder she's been in love for 30 years!

So with her dog cup running over, Nona has written five books on canine subjects, three of them on Goldens. The very first book garnered the coveted Dog Writer's Association of America Best Breed Book of the Year award, the first such award ever captured by her breed.

Nona believes that writing this book spurred her to brush up on dog stuff and minutiae that had slipped into her third memory bank—and that she learned new things along the way. If there's a dog lesson to be shared here, it's that we can never stop learning or know too much about our own Goldens or the canine universe.

Part 1

All That Glitters

So what is it about Golden Retrievers? How come we see their smiling faces on everything from dog food bags to sport utility vehicle commercials? Is it those melty deep brown eyes, that silly Golden grin, that sly come-hither look? Has the entire country gone to the dogs, specifically gone to Gold?

Before I rant and rave about living with pure gold and training it, you should have a good understanding of what the Golden Retriever is and what it is not. Just because you see one in every neighborhood doesn't mean the breed is right for everyone. True, they're great family dogs, keen competitors and dandy gun dogs, but no breed is perfect, and that includes the Golden.

Is a Golden Retriever right for you? Read on, and you'll find out. You already have a Golden pup? I repeat, read on, and you'll find out how to have a wonderful life together! Let's start your Golden tour, and you can decide for yourself.

Chapter 1

What's Gold About the Golden?

In This Chapter

➤ Golden Retrievers are good sports and great family dogs

➤ Color does not affect quality

➤ Goldens are not trained in the womb

If any dog is aptly named, it has to be the Golden Retriever. Especially the "golden" part. What began as a description of his yellow coat more appropriately describes his sunny disposition and his 14-karat value to his owner and society. This happy, funny, friendly fetcher of anything not nailed down has captured a permanent corner of the 1990s American heart, home, and marketplace.

So it's no accident that you see a smiling Golden Retriever in every magazine from *Vogue* to *Rolling Stone*. These big, blond beauties are the most popular advertising gimmicks of the '90s.Television loves their huggability as well as their trainability. What other dog can leap so high or smile so wide into that camera lens? As one of the American Kennel Club's five most popular dog breeds, Goldens are no doubt the most photographed subject in the media. Of course, dogophiles enjoy every minute of it, and even abnormal non-dog people will admit (under their breath) that they're kinda cute.

With all that hoopla, it's no big surprise you also see at least one in every neighborhood. Golden Retrievers are great family dogs and all-around good sports who think they were created purely to please their person. Give them a couch cushion with a human on it, a puddle to play in, and a stick or tennis ball to fetch and carry (maybe not in that order), and you've made their day. As a bonus, throw in an occasional duck or pheasant—after all, "retriever" is 50 percent of this dog's name!

Golden Roots

Our charismatic retriever is an immigrant, a hunting dog bred and born over 100 years ago in Scotland. To the Golden's credit, he has surpassed Scottish tweeds and kilts in popularity and today performs well beyond the duck blind he was born for. Overdosed with talent and versatility, the 20th century Golden consistently outperforms other breeds in every discipline in dog sports, including more mundane activities like sock and shoe theft. (Just ask my personal Golden Retriever crew about that!)

Do Blonds Really Have More Fun?

The color of that lush Golden Retriever coat dates back to the breed's four original yellow ancestors crossed with a few selected hunting breeds sprinkled here and there during the late 19th century. Today the breed color can range from very pale blond to reddish gold to deep Irish Setter red (pardon the non-Scottish comparison).

As Good as Gold

It's no coincidence that the Golden Retriever's personality is as golden as his outer coat. The Golden, bless his heart, was bred to please. He began as a hunting partner that delivered birds to hand and has evolved into modern times delivering whatever suits his owner's fancy. He's always happy to oblige. Remember those beer commercials on TV? These delightful retrievers live up to their names.

Bet You Didn't Know

The color of the Golden's coat has nothing to do with his intelligence or equally golden temperament. Color matters occasionally in the conformation ring. Show judges of the '90s seem to prefer blonds, which only means they probably spend too much time watching reruns of old Marilyn Monroe movies.

A Golden Partnership

Because Golden Retrievers were originally bred to work in tandem with a human, they are highly trainable, eager to please creatures who are a true blessing in this era of so many wild and crazy dogs who drive their owners nuts. That doesn't mean that they're born trained. It just means they're very willing fellows that like to work as a team, and if you're the captain of the team, your Golden will be delighted to do your bidding. Remember the part about the captain; it's important!

To Err Is Human; To Forgive Is Typically Golden

Goldens have the dog world's most forgiving disposition and will blithely dismiss all those dumb mistakes you're bound to make. Whether you come home two hours late, forget his dinner bowl, or accidentally step on his tail, he'll forget it ever happened once you smile at him. (A hefty scratch behind his ears, and he's your slave forever.) That does not imply that you have his permission to do stupid things. It just means he understands that you're only human.

Likewise, you should follow his good example and forgive your dog his trespasses. In dog terms, they're not mistakes because he's just a dog and the product of his instincts and your training, good or bad. I hate to be redundant, but that's another important statement to remember.

Goldens are known for their good looks and their easygoing disposition.

But surprise! Goldens are not for everyone. No breed of dog is perfect, although Golden Retrievers *do* come mighty close. Hopefully, you're one of those lucky people who is perfect for the breed.

The Least You Need to Know

➤ A Golden's coat color doesn't matter.

➤ Your Golden will love you unconditionally.

➤ Trainable means a Golden still requires training.

The Making of 14-Karat Dogs

A charming tale existed years ago about a group of Russian circus dogs that evolved into the very talented Golden Retriever.

Only an idiot would buy into that one. The truth is we can thank a Scotsman for our lovely breed. Sir Dudley Marjoriebanks (later elevated to Lord Tweedmouth and so named because his estate rested on the Tweed River in the hills of Inverness, Scotland) was an avid sportsman with a special passion for waterfowling. Apparently collecting the ducks he shot over those rough coastal waters wasn't easy, and he longed for a canine hunting companion who would not only swim out to retrieve his birds, but also deliver them to hand. And he had a yen for a yellow dog to do the job. Sounds like a good idea to me, too.

The Original Gold Nugget

So in 1868, Tweedmouth launched his first experimental yellow breeding, mating a liver-colored Tweed Water Spaniel (the name begs

no explanation) named Belle to a yellow Wavy-Coated Retriever
named Nous, which in Greek means wisdom. See anything prophetic
in that name? Nous was the only yellow pup, in those days called a
"sport," out of a litter of all black dogs, which was the standard color
for the Wavy-Coat.

Surprise! Nous and Belle produced four yellow furries, which
Tweedmouth promptly named Cowslip, Ada, Crocus, and Primrose.
He kept Cowslip for himself and gave the other pups to good friends
who shared his passion for breeding a yellow sporting dog.

Tweedmouth's kennel records show a detailed history of Color-Me-
Yellow canine marriages dating back to Cowslip and his littermates.
Line breeding (in which dogs of the same breed are mated with their
relatives, such as a dog to his granddam) of this nature was pretty
radical in those days, so Tweedmouth was a true vanguard of his
time.

Bet You Didn't Know

The Golden Retriever has what's called a "double" coat, a soft downy
undercoat to insulate him from the cold and heat, and a longer outer
coat of guard hairs. He sheds his undercoat twice a year, most heavily in
the spring. The resulting clouds of dog down all over the house can make
you tear out your hair as well.

Is a Red Golden Just an Oxymoron?

So where did our red-gold and rust-colored Goldens come from?
Enter the Red Setter, the Bloodhound, and the yellow Labrador.
Breeding reliable retrieving dogs also meant improving and preserv-
ing essential sporting qualities such as scenting ability and other
important hunting talents. So along the way these retriever pioneers
occasionally out-crossed their yellow dogs to other popular hunting
breeds. It's often said the Golden nose is one of its most famous
parts, and we can thank the Bloodhound cross for that.

Although Goldens are found all over the U.S., they are especially popular in the bird-rich northern states.

Welcome to America

The Goldens' destiny eventually took them across the Atlantic into the United States and Canada. In the early 1900s, British military officers and other professionals often traveled with their hunting dogs so they could do a little shooting on their business trips. Eventually, the dogs were established in the U.S., growing especially popular in the bird-rich areas of the northern states and coastal areas. The breed is still abundant in those states where pheasant stock is plentiful, and that Golden nose can track them down.

Tweedmouth really did his homework. His yellow retrievers had such sweet and winning personalities they just naturally wiggled their way into the house after a hard day of hunting. Always smiling, great with kids, and eager to please, the Golden was as good in the house as he was afield. By 1950, the breed was becoming well known as a dual-purpose dog.

Officially Golden

The American Kennel Club first recognized the Golden Retriever in 1925. By 1938 the breed had gained enough popularity that Golden

9

fanciers formed a national breed club. Thus was born the Golden Retriever Club of America to help direct the future of the breed in the United States. By the late 1990s, the GRCA had about 50 member clubs across the country.

Those local Golden Retriever clubs are a great resource for Golden Retriever owners. You don't have to be a canine expert or good at anything doggie to join a dog club. Just loving your dog like crazy is reason enough. You'll get lots of good dog advice and information from more experienced club members, and it's a great place to share the dog tales and brags that your other friends are sick of hearing.

The Let's-Do-It-All Dog

Golden Retrievers are natural athletes who have dipped their paws in every canine sporting discipline. They are joyful companions who are willing to try anything as long as they can enjoy it with someone fun to be with. Yes, some of them still hunt, too! However, to be fair to both dog and owner, urban sprawl has removed so many hunting areas and opportunities, it's tough to find a wild, much less legal, pheasant, duck, or goose within most city limits. But even birdless, this is still one happy dog that excels in all areas of dogdom. A dog as handsome, lovable, and talented as the Golden Retriever was destined to capture America's collective heart.

Gold Samaritans

Beyond sportsmanship, that famous Golden nose has nudged its way into almost every other facet of the human-animal connection. Today they serve their human masters as assistance dogs for the physically disabled, guide dogs for the blind, and hearing dogs for the deaf. And those Golden noses keep on sniffing, working for law enforcement as drug and arson detectives, and as search and rescue dogs who find victims buried under snow and earthquake rubble. Beyond that, they also excel as therapy dogs in hospitals and nursing homes where, unlike the average hourly employee, they love their jobs (just watch our Golden Retriever, Apache, race for the front door of the nursing home). And they work for free, unless you count dog biscuits as a paycheck.

Golden Paw Prints in the Ring and Field

Always great showmen and competitors, Goldens trip the light fantastic in the conformation ring, beguiling the judges and the spectators with their beauty and performance. Goldens consistently outshine all other breeds in the obedience ring, winning trials and wowing the audience with their high-stepping strut. And a lucky minority still pursue their birthright in the field, in hunting tests, field trials, and doing the real thing with their hunter-owners. Beyond even that, Goldens often steal the show at agility events and flyball competition. With all those fun activities, no wonder these Golden dogs are always smiling!

The Big Split

It was inevitable that a dog this versatile and talented would be embraced by sporting specialists and bred for specific qualities for various canine competitions. Today the conformation crowd breeds Goldens for their grand good looks, obedience enthusiasts prefer high-stepping Goldens that love teamwork, and the bird dog division looks for Goldens that still love birds and water.

As a result, there's often a huge difference in how each type of Golden looks and acts—Golden Retrievers all, but be careful which you choose. While each type should have a heart of gold, remember there are gold-plated and several varieties of solid gold.

The Least You Need to Know

➤ Goldens came from Scotland, not from circus dogs.

➤ The original Golden was a hunting dog.

➤ Goldens are want-to, can-do, do-it-all dogs.

➤ Most show Goldens are not hunting Goldens.

➤ Working Goldens seldom win in show rings.

Chapter 3

The Standard for the Golden Retriever

In This Chapter

➤ What is an AKC breed standard?

➤ The Golden Retriever coat, color, and temperament

➤ The Golden's body parts

All breeds must have a standard. Without one, you could breed a dog with big black or white spots to another spotted dog, and a few generations down the road you'd have a leopard-spotted Golden. That's what genetics is all about.

It's the job and purpose of every breed's parent club to decide how to preserve the purity of their chosen breed. Goldens were originally hunting dogs (Burn that picture in your brain!), and the standard says so. The standard also dictates other characteristics of the Golden, like its color, coat type, size, and temperament.

If you know these qualities, you'll be able to recognize a decent Golden when you see one. There are some poor quality animals out there, so you don't want to be an idiot about the breed standard.

A Golden Blueprint

The following is the standard as approved by the AKC. Just like the U.S. Constitution or other complex legal documents, it has its share of funny terms and language. We'll explain it (my explanations are in italic type) and define some of the dog descriptions later.

General Appearance

A symmetrical, powerful, active dog, sound and well put together, not clumsy nor long in leg, displaying a kindly expression and possessing a personality that is eager, alert, and self-confident. Primarily a hunting dog, he should be shown in hard-working condition. Overall appearance, balance, gait, and purpose to be given more emphasis than any of his component parts.

Faults: Any departure from the described ideal shall be considered faulty to the degree to which it interferes with the breed's purpose or is contrary to breed character.

Size, Proportion, Substance

Males 23–24 inches in height at withers (see "Neck, Topline, Body"); females 21½–22½ inches. Dogs up to one inch above or below standard size should be proportionately penalized. Deviation in height of more than one inch from standard shall disqualify.

Length from breastbone to point of buttocks slightly greater than height at withers in ratio of 12:11. Weight for dogs 65–75 pounds; bitches 55–65 pounds.

Head

Broad in skull, slightly arched laterally and longitudinally without prominence of frontal bones (*forehead*) or occipital bones (*top back point of the skull*). Stop (*between the eyes, where the top of the nose and forehead meet*) well defined but not abrupt. Foreface (*front of face*) deep and wide; nearly as long as skull. Muzzle straight in profile, blending smoothly and strongly into skull; when viewed in profile or from above, slightly deeper and wider at stop than at tip. No heaviness in flews (*the skin or flap that hangs from the dog's muzzle—or his lip*). Removal of whiskers is permitted but not preferred.

Eyes friendly and intelligent in expression, medium large with dark, close-fitting rims, set well apart and reasonably deep in sockets. Color preferably dark brown; medium brown acceptable. Slant eyes and narrow, triangular eyes detract from correct expression and are to be faulted. No white or haw *(lining inside the lower eye lid)* visible when looking straight ahead. Dogs showing evidence of functional abnormality of eyelids or eyelashes (such as, but not limited to, trichiasis, entropion, ectropion, or distichiasis) are to be excused from the ring.

Ears rather short with front edge attached well behind and just above the eye and falling close to cheek. When pulled forward, tip of ear should just cover the eye. Low, hound-like ear set to be faulted.

Nose black or brownish black, though fading to a lighter shade in cold weather not serious. Pink nose or one seriously lacking in pigmentation to be faulted.

Teeth scissors bite, in which the outer side of the lower incisors touches the inner side of the upper incisors. Undershot *(the lower front teeth protrude beyond the front upper teeth in bite or closed position)* or overshot *(just the opposite; the lower jaw is shorter, so the upper front teeth bite down over the lower teeth)* bite is a disqualification. Misalignment of teeth (irregular placement of incisors) or a level bite (incisors meet each other edge to edge) is undesirable, but not to be confused with undershot or overshot. Full dentition. Obvious gaps are serious faults.

Bet You Didn't Know

Your Golden's nose may turn a little pink in winter. Not to worry. It's called a "snow nose" and will turn black again in spring. Some dogs get it, and some don't. Others get it later in life; it depends on the dog. Don't worry about it.

Neck, Backline, Body

Neck medium long, merging gradually into well laid back shoulders, giving sturdy, muscular appearance. No throatiness. Backline strong and level from withers *(top of the shoulders, just behind the neck)* to slightly sloping croup *(the lower back, from the front of the pelvis to the base of the tail)*, whether standing or moving. Sloping backline, roach *(humped up)* or sway back, flat or steep croup to be faulted.

Body well balanced, short coupled *(not an excessively long body)*, deep through the chest. Chest between forelegs at least as wide as a man's closed hand including thumb, with well developed forechest *(top of the chest)*. Brisket *(lower chest under the breastbone extending to between the front legs)* extends to elbow. Ribs long and well sprung but not barrel shaped, extending well toward hindquarters. Loin *(from the rib cage to the pelvis)* short, muscular, wide, and deep, with very little tuck-up. Slab-sidedness *(a flat or caved-in chest)*, narrow chest, lack of depth in brisket, excessive tuck-up *(underneath the rear part of the body)* to be faulted.

Tail well set on, thick and muscular at the base, following the natural line of the croup. Tail bones extend to, but not below, the point of hock *(the joint between the lower thigh and rear pastern—sort of the rear elbow. . . see pasterns, next paragraph)*. Carried with merry action, level or with some moderate upward curve; never curled over back nor between the legs.

Forequarters

Muscular, well coordinated with hindquarters and capable of free movement. Shoulder blades long and well laid back with upper tips fairly close together at withers. Upper arms appear about the same length as the blades, setting the elbows back beneath the upper tip of the blades, close to the ribs without looseness. Legs, viewed from the front, straight with good bone, but not to the point of coarseness. Pasterns *(on the leg, just above the foot, where the foot, or wrist/carpus, bends into the leg. Metacarpus in front; metatarsus in rear)* short and strong, sloping slightly with no suggestion of weakness. Dewclaws *(a nail-bearing fifth toe on the inside of the front leg above the rest of the toes)* on forelegs may be removed, but are normally left on.

16

A Golden's legs should be straight, neither turned in nor out.
(Winter Churchill)

Feet medium size, round, compact, and well knuckled, with thick pads. Excess hair may be trimmed to show natural size and contour. Splayed *(the toes—or digits—are split apart or separated)* or hare feet *(center toes are more than a hair longer than the outer toes)* to be faulted.

Hindquarters

Broad and strongly muscled. Profile of croup slopes slightly; the pelvic bone slopes at a slightly greater angle (approximately 30 degrees from horizontal). In a natural stance, the femur *(thigh bone, rear leg)* joins the pelvis at approximately a 90-degree angle; stifles *(a joint in the thigh, sometimes called the knee)* well bent; hocks *(tarsus—the joint between the lower thigh and rear pastern)* well let down with short, strong rear pasterns. Feet as in front. Legs straight when viewed from rear. Cow hocks *(hind legs that bend in)*, spread hocks *(just the opposite)*, and sickle hocks *(hocks with angulation in sickle shape)* to be faulted.

Coat

Dense and water repellent with good undercoat. Outer coat firm and water resilient, neither coarse nor silky, lying close to the body; may be straight or wavy. Untrimmed natural ruff; moderate feathering on back of forelegs and on underbody; heavier feathering on front of neck, back of thighs, and underside of tail. Coat on head, paws, and front of legs is short and even. Excessive length, open coats, and limp, soft coats are very undesirable. Feet may be trimmed and stray hairs neatened, but the natural appearance of coat or outline should not be altered by cutting or clipping.

Color

Rich, lustrous golden of various shades. Feathering may be lighter than rest of coat. With the exception of graying or whitening of face or body due to age, any white marking, other than a few white hairs on the chest, should be penalized according to its extent. Allowable light shadings are not to be confused with white markings. Predominant body color which is either extremely pale or extremely dark is undesirable. Some latitude should be given to the light puppy whose coloring shows promising of deepening with maturity. Any noticeable area of black or other off-color hair is a serious fault.

Gait

When trotting, gait is free, smooth, powerful, and well coordinated, showing good reach. Viewed from any position, legs turn neither in nor out, nor do feet cross or interfere with each other. As speed increases, feet tend to converge toward centerline of balance. It is recommended that dogs be shown on a loose lead to reflect true gait.

Temperament

Friendly, reliable, and trustworthy. Quarrelsomeness or hostility towards other dogs or people in normal situations, or an unwarranted show of timidity or nervousness, is not in keeping with Golden Retriever character. Such actions should be penalized according to their significance.

Disqualifications

Deviation in height of more than one inch from standard either way.

Undershot or overshot bite.

Bet You Didn't Know

Check out the dog on the tear-card of this book to find canine body parts you don't understand. Not to diminish the value of the standard, but unless you're showing your dog in conformation, you won't need to study this chapter any further. A good breeder should have sound representatives of the breed.

The Least You Need to Know

➤ The Golden is primarily a hunting dog, not just a fluffy couch potato.

➤ A breed standard is necessary to preserve a breed's integrity..

➤ Dogs who seriously deviate from the standard may make good pets but shouldn't be bred.

19

Chapter 4

Golden Retriever Fever

In This Chapter

➤ Living with big, hairy, happy dogs

➤ Dog hair on your dinner plate

➤ Training is not just important; it's a must

➤ It takes two to exercise

➤ Gold is a long-term investment

Of course you want a Golden Retriever. What person in their right mind wouldn't? And you firmly believe you and the dog would be a Golden combination.

Well, maybe. Despite their high profile status in the media, Goldens aren't for everyone. This is a sporting breed, folks. These are high-energy dogs who require training to learn good manners and appropriate behavior (the same requirements as most dogs, actually). Because Goldens are easily trained and love to learn, this could and should be a fun but very busy experience. But before you trot down the yellow brick road, let's talk about the pitfalls as well as the pleasures of Golden Retrieverdom.

Panning for Gold

You have a major case of Golden Retriever puppy fever. No, that's not a dog disease. It's a people condition that most often occurs in spring when humans become infected with an uncontrollable urge to add a puppy to the family. It can lead to dog heaven or, heaven forbid, a nervous breakdown if the affected person thinks all Goldens are like the ones they see on television. The cure, getting that cute puppy immediately, can be worse than the disease. If you're serious about this Golden business and not just caving in to the kids or some other wild and crazy impulse, follow the advice of responsible dog owners and breeders. Look deep into your dog-loving soul and check out the big picture. Love alone is not enough.

Growing Up, and Up, and Up

Goldens are big, sprawling dogs that easily occupy at least one couch cushion or easy chair. Everything's big, including their muddy paw prints on your kitchen floor and their nose prints on the window. That happy Golden tail will easily clear your coffee table. (Sorry, move your Waterford.) They need space, and lots of it, both in the house and out. A yard is a must, good fencing preferred.

Dog Hair as a Condiment

These are hairy critters. They shed their downy undercoat in huge quantities every spring and drip a little dog hair all over the house all year long. Even fastidious Golden owners learn to pick dog hair out of their teeth and tolerate it in their soup and salad. It's no coincidence that Golden owners never wear black or navy blue.

Brushing will help keep that nuisance dog hair to a minimum. Daily brushing is best; twice weekly is a must. If you use a professional groomer, expect to pay $15 to $25 per grooming session. Pretty is seldom cheap.

Exercise Nourishes the Canine Mind and Body

A normal Golden usually creates a little happy chaos, which is part of his irresistible appeal. These are spirited dogs with a great sense of humor who love to retrieve, play, chase, and chew. They need exercise to expend all that sporting energy, or they will entertain themselves mischievously (destructively). The typical Golden Retriever household usually has ragged chew marks on a few chair legs, dog bones strewn about the living room, and piles of shredded sticks in the back yard.

Your Golden will not exercise without you. You are his incentive to romp and play. Daily walks and jogs, Frisbee games, and bumper chasing (those large, hot-dog shaped canvas or plastic retrieving objects sold in pet stores for retrieve-a-holic dogs) will help keep your Golden tired, content, and physically fit.

Goldens Love to Go Along

Are you an active family who loves the outdoor life? Are you able or willing to take your Golden to soccer practice and baseball games? If you're on the go and never home and he's alone most of the day, your Golden will be stressed and most unhappy. That's not fair to the dog and could be calamitous for you. Goldens need to be with people, and an isolated and lonely Golden can easily suffer from separation anxiety, which will lead to destructive behavior. It's a natural canine stress reliever.

More Than 10 Minutes a Day

As in exercise, a Golden Retriever will not train himself. Good manners are not included in his pedigree. It's up to you, the team captain, to teach your dog acceptable behavior, what he may and may not do at home and in the neighborhood. Obedience training is the only way to accomplish that. Few pet owners have the know-how, expertise, or motivation to do it solo, so training classes must be part of your Golden agenda. That also means practicing every day, or your once-a-week classes will be wasted.

Don't be misled by the overused 10-minutes-a-day obedience slogan. That might apply to the "Sit" or "Stay" command, but training is an ongoing process whenever you're with your dog and he's awake. If you can't or won't commit to raising your Golden as you would an infant or toddler, don't blame your Golden if he's wild or disobedient. Better think about getting a stuffed animal instead.

Golden Goodies

If you're looking for a guard dog, get rid of this book and investigate another breed. Most Goldens are complete love sponges that would happily lick the boots of an intruder. You can encourage them to bark at people who approach your house, but you can't—and should-n't—teach them to intimidate or bite. Their very size might deter a home invader, but anyone familiar with a Golden's love-'em-all attitude knows that a scratch behind Golden ears means instant friendship.

On the other hand, I firmly believe that my Golden family would sense any danger to me personally and would defend me to the death. Stories abound about Golden Retriever heroes who have protected children and adults who were in danger or threatened by some adversary.

Kids + Puppies = Chaos

Back again to active families. How old are your children? If your kids are under three and you get a puppy, you will now have the equivalent of two or three kids under three! Double your pleasure and, you got it, twice the work. And a major communication problem. Because neither pup nor child has learned the house rules yet, almost everything they hear will be a No-No, which creates a negative learning environment for both child and dog. Puppies nip and chew; kids pull tails and sit on furry bodies. Both require 24-hour attention. And let's face it, when you have to prioritize, the puppy naturally loses. That's not fair to the dog. Some breeders will insist you wait until your child is older before they let you have one of their prize packages. My personal age limit is three years old. The breeder philosophy is "Your kid, my puppy." Just looking out for Numero Uno.

All Goldens Are Not Created Equal

Don't let all this talk about active, high-energy Golden Retrievers discourage you. You can still find a quiet(er) Golden companion that won't disrupt your household. Some lines (or families) of show-type Goldens produce a more laid-back animal that doesn't act like Robocop. Look in Chapter 5, "Finding a Breeder Who Is Golden," for more details.

Goldens are great family dogs; adult dogs are best for very young children. (Dennis Gray)

Worth His Weight in Gold

You have to think long term when you consider gold. Food, veterinary care, and training, possibly doggie day care, can have a major impact on your budget. And there are no "laters" or "maybes." A sick dog, like a sick child, needs attention now, not when you have the money. In both the short term and the long haul, dogs, especially large ones, add up to megabucks. So before you fall in love with some blond cutie, be sure you can afford it.

The Least You Need to Know

➤ Expect to live with dog hair in your house and swimming pool.

➤ Goldens are large dogs who need brushing and lots of exercise.

➤ You can't leave your Golden puppy alone all day.

➤ Train your Golden, or he won't act like a canine good citizen.

➤ Owning a Golden is expensive.

➤ Owning a Golden is worth all of the above!

Part 2

Going for the Gold

All systems are go; a Golden it will be. You've made a smart decision (and who should know better than myself with 30 Golden years behind me). Now follow along and learn to shop smart when you search for a good breeder; smart puppy buyers end up with good breeders and smart puppies!

Then we'll go shopping (Oh joy!) for all that cute and necessary doggy stuff. We'll make your house and garden puppy-safe and discuss how to plan a safe and happy welcome home. We'll even fix him up with his own little doggy den and help you deal with potty breaks. That's a lot to digest at one time, so grab a chair, get comfy, and let's chat.

Chapter 5

Finding a Breeder Who Is Golden

In This Chapter

➤ AKC myths and foibles

➤ Pedigrees are canine family trees

➤ Dissecting your dog's pedigree

➤ Profile of a reputable breeder

➤ How good breeders raise their pups

Humans have family trees; dogs have pedigrees. Just as our ancestry could include bank robbers or other unsavory people, so too can a dog's pedigree contain some very common, even crummy, parents, grandparents, aunts, or uncles. And their genetic influence will determine what kind of dog your Golden will grow up to be. So when you're looking for a Golden, pedigree is the first order of the day.

Good breeders build good pedigrees. Next logical conclusion, a good breeder will be the most important ingredient in your puppy search. How do you find one? What do you ask, and, likewise, what should they ask you? (If a breeder doesn't ask you questions, hang up the phone or leave the premises. End of story.) Scrutinize the breeder's expertise and puppy-raising skills. Be careful if those little fuzzballs are not her first priority. A good breeder is very protective of her protégé.

Papers as in AKC

The American Kennel Club is among other things a central registry of dogs, and "papers" are their confirmation of a puppy's parents.

We've all heard those famous dog words, "Of course, he's a good dog; he's AKC." Or "He's a good dog; he has all his papers," or "He's pure-bred; his parents were AKC."

Don't buy into that. Papers and AKC-registered have absolutely nothing to do with a dog's quality or worth. They mean one thing only: that the dog's parents were recognized by AKC as being of the same breed. What it does not prove or guarantee is that those parents, or their offspring, were healthy, sound, stable, or even fair quality animals.

Pedigree Analysis

An AKC registration form and a pedigree are two different documents. The registration is simply AKC's confirmation of a puppy's sire and dam and certifies you as the owner of that pup. It is *not* the dog's pedigree, which is a three to five generation list of all its ancestors. Let's start with mom and dad and research your Golden's pedigree.

The sire and dam are your dog's father and mother. In the next generation, we have two granddams and two grandsires, and so on up the pedigree ladder. There may be titles before and/or after certain dogs' names, indicating some great or small accomplishment in a particular area of the dog world.

Titles = Royalty

A breeder may tell you her dog is smart, beautiful or handsome, has lots of talent, and so on, but how do you know that's true? Titles in a pedigree prove it. There's a complete list of titles in the Appendix A, and these titles are also explained more fully in the chapters on breed activities.

This does not mean if a pedigree lacks titles, the puppies have no potential as competitors or pets. But unless the breeder is very experienced and knows what she's doing, a nondescript pedigree offers little assurance that the pups are top quality Goldens.

Healthy Choices

The sire and dam of any Golden litter you consider should carry the standard health clearances for hips, eyes, heart, and if at all possible, elbows. All those dog parts can be defective, and if either parent has hip dysplasia, cataracts, heart disease, or elbow disorders, it's a good bet they could pass that condition along to their pups. These diseases are discussed further in Chapter 20, "Hereditary Diseases," but this quick overview will help you out.

Good and Bad Joints

An updated or current AKC registration will show an OFA rating after a dog's name, indicating it has been declared free of hip dysplasia by the Orthopedic Foundation for Animals (OFA), which is the official hip clearing house for dogs. Example: Dam: Chances R Gingersnap, SF123456 (AKC registration number) (8-98) (date of evaluation) OFA24E (OFA rating). In OFA language, there are three levels of non-dysplastic hips. The letter *E* indicates a rating of Excellent, *G* means Good, and *F* is Fair. Dysplastic ratings of mild, moderate, and severe indicate the degree of hip dysplasia and will not appear on the registra-

Doggy Don'ts

Steer clear of the breeder who tells you her dog doesn't need a hip clearance because he or she can jump a six-foot fence in one great leap. Or one who tells you the pups are from "championship lines" when in fact there's only one solitary Ch. title three generations back.

tion. OFA ratings were not recorded with AKC prior to the 1990s, so the breeder will have to produce OFA certificates if the dog's AKC registration certificate lacks an OFA clearance. OFA also certifies elbows, and because elbow disease has become so common (see the section on elbow disorders in Chapter 20), many breeders include elbow clearances on their breeding stock.

The Eyes Have It

Pedigrees may also show CERF numbers that indicate the eye clearance is registered with the Canine Eye Registry Foundation. However, many dogs with eye clearance certificates are not registered with

CERF, so their pedigrees will not reflect that status. In those cases, the breeder should be able to produce a board-certified ophthalmologist certificate stating that both parents' eyes have been examined and found to be free of hereditary cataracts.

Have a Heart

Yup, you'll need another letter of approval, this time from a board-certified cardiologist stating that both parents' hearts were tested and found to be free of a heart disease called SAS. (Sub-valvular Aortic Stenosis). More on SAS in Chapter 20.

Bet You Didn't Know

If you're lucky and find health clearances on a puppy's grandparents and other ancestors, all the better. One fact will always hold true. The stronger the gene pool, the healthier the offspring.

Happy Parents, Happy Pups

Good temperament also is inherited. (Okay, let's face it. Just about everything good—or bad—is inherited.) If the sire or dam or other close relative is aggressive with other dogs or even people, it's a good bet some of the puppies will reflect those qualities. When you visit a litter of pups, interact with one or both parents if you can. Quite frequently the sire lives elsewhere, but the dam is surely present. If the breeder won't let you meet the mom, or either mom or dad is surly or growly, overly shy or slinky, look elsewhere for a pup. Good litters are worth waiting for.

More Than Just a Breeder

If you don't already have a breeder reference from someone you know and trust, you might want to ask this breeder about previous litters and where you can meet other dogs that she's bred and the people who own them.

Breeders Grill Their Clients

A reputable breeder would be more than willing to offer references as well as all the previous information without being asked to do so. In fact, she may give you more details than you want or need to know. That's great, because it means she knows her dog facts and wants to make you dog-smart, too, especially if you're going to raise one of her little Golden gems. The breeder will also want to know about your family, the ages of your kids, and who will be home to raise the puppy. Some insist on meeting all family members before sending a puppy home. (I do.) Don't be offended; she's not being nosy. It's just your typical job interview.

Breeders Are Brutally Honest

Reputable breeders also should tell you what's good and what's not so good about living with a Golden Retriever. No breed of dog is perfect, and the breeder should volunteer the disadvantages of Golden ownership (like shedding, size, and energy level) along with all the happy news.

Bet You Didn't Know

Most breeders who raise competition Goldens have "pet quality" pups from every litter. A good quality pet Golden Retriever will cost from $350 to $600. That $200 Golden pup is not a bargain and could end up costing a fortune in medical bills, not to mention heartbreak.

Signing on the Dotted Line

Most breeders have puppy contracts that specify health guarantees and some agreement or arrangement to take the puppy back or refund your purchase price if the pup fails to meet the health guarantees in the contract. The contract should include a spay/neuter clause and indicate if the pup is being sold on a limited registration. See Appendix C for details on limited registrations.

These puppies are three weeks old and need another month with their dam and litter-mates for proper socialization. A good breeder will not let a puppy leave her home until he is at least seven weeks old.

The True Hobby Breeder

There are several things responsible breeders do not do. They don't keep several different breeds of dogs on premises that spend their entire lives in pens, cages, or kennels, popping out puppies every year. Good Golden breeders are dedicated—no, fanatics—about their breed. Their dogs are members of the family and usually live in the house (at least most of the time) and enjoy the same privileges as the kids. (Okay, maybe they don't all sleep on the bed like mine do.) These same Golden breeders breed no more than one or two litters a year. In fact, one litter a year is more the norm. Make sure any breeder you consider fits that description!

Be a Retriever Detective: How Do You Find This Walk-on-Water Breeder?

How do you find a solid Golden breeder you can trust?

No Newspaper Ads

For starters, a wise puppy shopper will *not* look in the newspaper want ads. Good breeders seldom advertise. They usually have reservations in advance and depend on referrals from other dog friends or previous puppy clients. They also don't want to interview hundreds of people to find proper homes for their puppies and will keep puppies past the normal seven-to-eight-week placement age until the right person comes along.

Ask Your Veterinarian

Your veterinarian may be able to recommend a reputable Golden owner or breeder. If you don't have or know a vet, ask a friend's vet.

Ask Other Golden Owners

Talk to people who own Goldens you admire and ask them where they got their dog. Be careful with this. Of course they love their Golden, but they may have found him through a want ad or other questionable source. You don't want to take that chance.

Go to Dog Events

Spend the day at a dog show, an obedience show, or field event. You'll see a wide variety of Goldens and can get up close and personal with the ones you like. Most dog owners who show their dogs in the various dog activities enjoy nothing better than talking about their special Goldens and where they got them.

Clubs Are Good Sources

Check with a local kennel club or dog training club. You can also call or write to the AKC, 260 Madison Ave., New York, NY 10016, for contacts in the Golden Retriever Club of America. These contacts can refer you to a Golden breeder in your area.

The Least You Need to Know

➤ A Golden pup will resemble his Golden ancestors.

➤ An intelligent puppy search will produce a quality pup.

➤ Breeders and buyers should quiz each other.

➤ A good breeder is particular about who buys her pups.

➤ A good breeder is worth her weight in gold.

Chapter 6

A Golden Match

> ### In This Chapter
>
> ➤ What are your Golden hopes and dreams
>
> ➤ Picking the perfect pup
>
> ➤ Leave your wallet and the kids at home

The breeder is only 50 percent of your perfect puppy combination. The right puppy is the other half. Before you start your puppy search, be sure you know exactly what kind of Golden Retriever you're looking for. Remember that big split we talked about a while ago? There's a Golden Retriever to suit almost every lifestyle. Choose wisely, and you'll end up in GR heaven. The wrong selection can lead to—let's not even talk about it.

In this chapter, I'll help you decide what kind of Golden will be best for you. Forewarned is forearmed. It's easy to fall in love with the first pretty face you see. Let's talk about how to avoid that trap.

Golden Images

First, close your eyes and say "Golden Retriever." What kind of Golden do you see, and what is that dog doing? Is it a lean, red-gold athlete leaping for a Frisbee or chasing the kids along the beach? Is it a furry blond sprawled in front of the fireplace, maybe snoozing on the couch? What kind of a Golden do you dream of living with?

➤ Do you hunt, or would you like to?

You'll need to research field and hunting lines to find a Golden who can share your duck blind and shag those pheasants from the fields and hedgerows.

➤ Are you a sports nut, a camping enthusiast, or a dedicated jogger?

You probably want a typical spirited Golden who would fit well into your outdoor activities.

➤ Are you a sedentary person who spends most of your leisure time curled up with a good book? Are you a senior citizen who wants a Golden mostly for its huggability?

You don't need a high-powered Golden that craves action and would be bouncing off the walls from boredom. Better to look for a laid-back animal, possibly from show lines, where the breeder's priorities lean more toward looks than to athletics.

Down the Yellow Brick Road

How about your long-term goals, other than family companion for the next 10 to 15 years? Are you interested in obedience trials, hunting tests, the conformation ring? Whatever your dreams or goals, there's a Golden breeder out there somewhere with pups to suit your fancy.

Be specific when looking for your ideal Golden. If the breeder raises field-type Goldens and you want a career in conformation, look elsewhere for your pup. The reverse is also true.

Dreams vs. Reality

Are your golden goals realistic? Consider what you can reasonably do compared to what you'd like to do. Sometimes these two add up to only one. (Okay, so I'm a writer, not a mathematician.) Often, the real world gets in the way of what we wish and what we actually can accomplish.

The Male vs. Female Dilemma

Is there a difference? Very little; both make excellent pets. Differences are more in the nature of individual personality than of gender. Males of course will be about 10 to 15 pounds bigger, therefore stronger, and may display more dominant behavior unless they're neutered at an early age. And they do lift their leg when urinating, putting your prize shrubs and flower beds at risk. Some males also take a little longer to mature, stretching their teen-age rowdiness into their second year, while females tend to become ladylike before they're two. There are major disadvantages with intact dogs of either sex, so spay/neuter as soon as your veterinarian recommends it. See Chapter 18 for more details on spaying and neutering.

If you already have an adult dog of any breed, it might be best to get a dog of the opposite sex from your present dog. Males tend to get into dominance wars at certain life stages, and dogs of opposite sexes usually cohabit better.

Be Prepared

When you launch your breeder-puppy search, compile a list of questions and all the dog details we've talked about so far. Forewarned is forearmed! Those little yellow fuzzballs will steal your heart with one sweet puppy kiss, and suddenly you own one. Unless you are absolutely positive this is *the* litter, don't fall in love with the first one who licks your cheek (Yeah, right!) and try to visit more than one litter. That's the only way to learn the differences in Golden personalities and how each breeder raises them. Remember, all Goldens are not created equal.

Checking Out the Breeder

The puppy environment is one important indicator of the breeder's level of care and expertise.

Where and How Are the Puppies Raised?

They should be in the house or an adjoining room, not isolated down in a basement or corner of the garage. (The key word here is *isolated*.) They need to be near family areas where they can be raised

Pick me!
(Winter Curchill)

and socialized with people every day, or they'll be fearful and intimidated by humans. The greater their exposure to household sights and sounds between four and seven weeks of age, the easier the transition from canine family to human family. *Socialize* is a word you'll hear often from now on. It all starts in the whelping box.

Puppy Hygiene

The puppy area should be reasonably clean, considering the non-stop food chain in a litter of healthy pups. What goes in keeps coming out all day long, so scrupulously clean is pretty tough, but your overall impression of "clean" is a good clue.

Puppy Appearance

The puppies themselves should have clean, thick coats and feel solid and muscular. No crusted or runny discharge from their eyes, ears, or nose. No watery or bloody stools. Their dewclaws should have been removed soon after birth, and they should have had one or two wormings and a parvo-distemper shot before seven weeks of age and before they leave their litter.

Color Him Gold—or Purple—or Blue

Breeders often use some form of identification when each pup is born. Colored rickrack ribbon is popular and happens to be my own preferred method. Newborn pups resemble a pile of skinny wet rodents, and color-coding is the easiest way to know at a glance which pup is the most aggressive eater and always at the best end of mom's dinner table, and which one does something first or last. When I have a litter, our normal puppy conversation is always about what Pink or Blue or Orange did today.

The puppies can't go home until they're 7 to 10 weeks old, depending on the breeder's policy. Most breeders release their puppies at about seven weeks of age. (If the breeder lets them go at five or six weeks, say goodbye and leave.) Breeders usually allow visitors after the pups are three or four weeks old, but you can't tell much about individual personality until they're at least five weeks of age. You can, however, get to know the breeder and the momma Golden in the meantime and decide if you want to join her Golden family.

Puppy Selection

Who's the fairest of them all? How do you know which one is the one, the pup who will fit into your family scheme of things just like a glove? Listen to your breeder. Her observations are often good criteria in evaluating puppies. After all, she has spent the last seven weeks living 24 hours a day with her furry charges and can point out the alpha pup, the middle of the road guys, and a shy, quiet wallflower if there is one. She can help you match a puppy to your goals and lifestyle.

The Puppy Test Debate

Breeder expertise aside, many people still rely on puppy tests. Puppy testing is certainly not a science and is a questionable art at best. Test results are influenced by so many factors: what person performs the test, where the test occurs, the time of day, if pups are hungry, tired, reacting to immunizations—you get the picture. And puppies mature at different rates, with one pup precocious at five or six weeks, while a littermate may not blossom until several days later. Many experts discount test results and remind us that some of the great dogs of our time have been leftover pups the breeder either gave away or kept because no one wanted them.

Bet You Didn't Know

A Golden puppy's ears are often slightly to moderately darker than the rest of his coat. The ear color is the best indicator of the color of his future adult coat. Some coats will take a year or longer to reach their permanent adult Golden hue.

Keep Detailed Test Results

When testing puppies, record a detailed description of their reactions (tail up, body crouched down, and so on) as well as a numerical grade. It will help you to remember why you gave a particular score as well as help you to interpret each reaction. This is especially important when you're testing a large litter. It's easy to forget what puppy Number Two did an hour ago, and scores alone don't tell you exactly in what manner each puppy reacted to the stimulus.

Puppy SATs

The first series of tests illustrated are the most widely used among hobby breeders. The second set of two tests is recommended by obedience and field trial competitors. Those two happen to be my personal favorites. But as with all things doggie, there are no guarantees. Be familiar with the stated reactions in the following scoring section before you start the scoring process.

1. **Attraction.**

   The breeder takes the puppy to a quiet testing area and places him down about 10 feet from the tester. The tester squats down and claps her hands while bending toward the pup, saying nothing. Observe how the puppy approaches the tester and score according to the chart later in the chapter.

2. **Handling.**

Now the tester should stroke the puppy from head to tail for about 30 seconds. Again record the pup's response and assign a score.

3. **Holding or cradle test.**

The tester picks up the pup and cradles him upside down with all four legs skyward, in her arms for about 20 to 30 seconds and scores accordingly.

4. **Following.**

The tester releases the puppy and stands up, then walks away without a word. If the pup follows, the tester chats with him to see if he will come along. If he doesn't follow at all, keep walking for a few more feet to see if he'll finally come along. Allow about one minute for this test and score accordingly.

Puppy Test Scores

Attraction	Score
Comes at once, bites or nips at your hands or feet	1
Comes quickly, licks but does not nip or bite	2
Comes slowly but without hesitation or shyness	3
Comes reluctantly or not at all, sits and observes instead	4
Does not come; turns and goes the other way	5
Handling	Score
Nips, growls, becomes agitated or excited	1
Jumps up happily, paws up, no nipping or biting	2
Wiggles around, licks at your hand	3
Rolls over on its back	4
Slinks away or walks away	5

Holding/Cradling	Score
Struggles fiercely, nips, bites, or growls	1
Struggles, then settles down or wiggles happily	2
Settles down first, then wiggles or struggles	3
Does not resist or struggle at all	4
Wiggles a little the entire time	5

Following	Score
Chases your feet, jumps on you or your feet, nips or bites	1
Follows happily, stays with you	2
Follows willingly but slowly	3
Does not follow; sits and watches	4
Does not follow; walks away	5

What the Numbers Mean

1. This is an extremely dominant and aggressive pup with a strong and willful personality. He will require a very experienced trainer who must be prepared for constant challenges to authority. This puppy will not be good with children and will need expert socialization by a very dominant owner. Not recommended for the average pet or companion home.

2. Also a dominant pup who will require a strong leader with experience and consistent training to become a reliable family companion.

3. Middle-of-the-road pup who is outgoing and friendly and will respond well to people and children. Will need more praise for confidence.

4. This pup is quite submissive and may not socialize too easily. It would need a gentle hand and long-term confidence building. Probably not a good choice for children.

5. This pup is terribly shy and would resist training. Pups with too many 5s are potential fear biters and seldom make good companion dogs.

These numerical categories are guidelines. Combination scores with 2s and 3s or 3s and 4s also make good family dogs. And remember, tests do not always reflect many aspects of the puppy's character.

The Competition Pup

The next two exercises are popular with the competition crowd. These tests should also be conducted by a stranger.

Confidence and Courage Test

Set up a large non-skid-surface table in a quiet area or a room that is completely new and foreign to the pup. The tester should carry the pup and place it on the table without a spoken word. Gauge the pup's reaction according to the scoring chart below.

Confidence and Courage Responses

Happy and fearless; tries to run around or jump off table	1
Tail high and wagging, investigates table, shows no fear	2
Tail wags slowly, curious but apprehensive, may crouch a bit, sniffs to investigate	3
Tail down or tucked under but wagging slightly, slinky, rather fearful, sniffs or investigates with much caution	4
Tail between hind legs, freezes and won't move, does not sniff or investigate	5

1. Pups that score 1–2 are bold, courageous, and outgoing, and will accept challenges and training with enthusiasm. These are good choices for competition or a busy, active family.

2. Scores of 3–4 are less confident puppies that would make good companions but will need more careful socializing and confidence building in their training. They will require a gentler, more patient hand in training.

3. A score of 5 indicates a pup that is insecure and will require lots of extra TLC and training to become a happy, willing worker and family member. May not be good with young children.

Desire to Retrieve Test

The tester should take the puppy to an unfamiliar area and set it down without a word. Make sure the area is clear of all distractions, toys, paper, or anything that could attract its attention. The tester then teases the puppy with a dead bird or some highly visible retrieving object like a stuffed white sock. When the puppy is all excited, the tester tosses the sock (at the pup's eye level) about six to eight feet in front of the puppy.

Grade the pup's intensity and desire to retrieve and score on 1 to 3 as described in the following paragraph. The tester should call the puppy to return with the object, but the return does not affect the test results. Coming back is a response that can be taught as the puppy grows. The desire to retrieve is built into the pup genetically.

Desire to Retrieve Responses

The puppy goes wild at the sight of the bird or sock bumper and strains madly to retrieve it when it's thrown.	1
The puppy shows enthusiasm for the bird or sock and runs out happily to retrieve it.	2
The puppy shows little interest in the retrieve object and merely wanders out to get it or fails to go at all.	3

1. Puppies who score 1 should make good hunters and good performers in field or obedience competition.

2. Puppies with a score of 2 should be adequate performers and with proper training and encouragement can reach competent levels of performance.

3. Do not consider a 3 for any type of hunting or retrieving activities other than a Frisbee game. While some pups' talent develops slowly with maturity, if you're hoping to enjoy hunting, hunt tests, or field trials, you need to narrow the field as much as possible. A promising puppy increases your odds of success in adventurous activities.

Remember that by the time you test puppy number 9, the testing area has been compromised with lots of puppy scent, and the early pups tested may be more wide awake and energetic than the last. The test results should be only one part of your puppy selection process.

You should also observe the puppies within the litter as much as possible to see which one is the boss pup, which one seems precocious, which one is the most inquisitive, and the like. If your breeder is involved in any type of performance competition, rely also on her evaluation of each pup.

One Is Fun

Let's suppose you've narrowed your choices down to two adorable pups. Because you can't decide which one, maybe you'll take both.

Doggy Do's

Base your decision about which puppy to bring home on a variety of factors: the information provided from the breeder, your own observations of the puppies together, and, if you have the puppies tested, on the test results. No one test or comment should be decisive.

Not! I agree with the experts who advise against the two-puppy household. No offense to you intended, but a puppy will always prefer the company of another pup to you. It's species selection, and your personal charm is not involved. Two puppies will form their own labor union, and you will be left out. Besides, you're not getting a puppy to provide a buddy for another pup. You want one for yourself!

There's another weighty argument against a two-pup household. The more dominant puppy will assert itself over the submissive one and could even develop a bully personality. These patterns of behavior can magnify over time, and it will be harder to train either pup. Naturally your puppy must learn how to behave around other dogs, but the two-puppy household is not the way to accomplish that. You're after that special human-canine bond.

If you control your urge for double trouble, you can decide later to become a two-Golden household, as so many Golden owners do. Wait until your dog is two years old before getting a second pup. By then Golden #1 will be your soul mate. However, raising puppy #2 will be a different challenge, as you'll have to separate the two dogs for at least six months to create an equally strong bond between you and the second dog. In my personal dog household, I keep a puppy with me almost exclusively until he's at least six months old. He might get a free period of 10 minutes a day two or three times a week with my adult Goldens, but I want him to bond to me. As a result, he will hear my voice in the middle of a traffic jam.

The Least You Need to Know

➤ Decide what kind of Golden you want before you look at pups.

➤ Screen your breeder carefully before you buy.

➤ The breeder's observations can help you pick your pup.

➤ One pup at a time; two pups are double trouble.

Chapter 7

Stocking the Puppy Larder

In This Chapter

➤ Your puppy shopping spree

➤ Collars, leashes, and long lines

➤ Toys—to chew and not to chew

➤ Great crates

Welcome to the wonderful world of Golden Retrievers! This is an exciting time, and your pre-puppy preparations are not only fun but very important to your puppy's welfare once he's home.

Puppy-proof your entire premises from the ground up, indulge your whimsy at the puppy store, and give your kids a short course in canine safety. Build this special pup a gilded cage!

Your Puppy's Necessities

Just like outfitting a newborn baby, your puppy will need his own layette of necessities and niceties. But I warn you, shopping for puppies is a grand adventure and can easily spin out of control—and out of your budget. Make a list of must-haves and another list of extra goodies so you know where to draw the line.

You really don't need a pull-toy to transport your puppy around the yard. . . but you might just want to indulge yourself, too.

Food and Water Bowls

Stainless steel bowls are best. They're indestructible and easy to sanitize. Buy the two-quart size for your future adult Golden. No need for tiny puppy pans; they outgrow them in a blink. If you lean toward fancy heavy stoneware bowls, think about your back and how often you'll have to pick it up. Plastic bowls are too flimsy and do not sanitize well.

Puppy Food

Be sure to ask your breeder what your puppy has been eating and if she can calculate approximately how much. (That can be difficult when eight or nine puppies are sharing one large food pan.) Lay in your own supply of a large-breed growth puppy food (see Chapter 21 on Nutrition for why this is so important). If the breeder has been feeding something different, take home a small bag of her food to mix with your new food so your puppy can adjust gradually to the change in diet. Start with 20 pounds of food. Does that sound like a lot? It won't last long!

Collars and ID Tags

For immediate daily use, purchase a narrow, adjustable nylon webbed collar with a plastic quick-release buckle. This will expand two to three inches in length as the puppy grows. The 8-to-12-inch size will fit your little pup, but not for long. Your Golden puppy will grow faster than your crabgrass. You'll replace this collar at least twice during his first year.

No chain or training collars on your puppy. Maybe when he's four or five months old. Those collars are for training purposes *only* and should never be worn beyond a training session. Tales abound about dogs who have been hanged or have choked themselves to death when their chain collars tangled on furniture or a fence post. You'll find lots more detail on collars in Chapter 14.

Attach a temporary identification tag to the puppy's collar. Never include the dog's name—a thief could call the pup using his name—just use your own name, address, and telephone number. Once he is fully grown and wears a collar he won't outgrow, rivet a brass ID plate on the collar instead of the standard S-hook dangle tag (plates are available through pet supply catalogs). Dangle tags get caught on carpeting and come off easily. The riveted plates are permanent and never snag. On my own ID plates, I include my telephone number on the name line and use the fourth line for the message, "Dog needs medication." If the dog is stolen, a thief might think twice about the value of a dog that has some sickness or disease. If he's lost, that health information might motivate whoever finds the dog to return him promptly. Can't hurt; might help.

Doggy Do's

Use an "O" ring (key chain ring) instead of the standard "S" hook to attach the tags to your dog's collar. The "S" hooks detach too easily. Convert to a riveted ID plate once the dog is wearing an adult-size collar.

Leashes

You always thought a leash was just a leash. For training purposes and control, you'll need an entire wardrobe of "lines" with which to lead your dog.

➤ A four-to-six-foot nylon leash. This will do nicely for your pup.

➤ A narrow six-foot leather lead. You'll need this size for obedience class in a few weeks. Purchase both leads before you bring your puppy home.

➤ A 16-to-20-foot expandable (flexi) lead. This is both convenient and necessary for outdoor walks and playtime. I always have two: one for the house and one in the truck so I won't inadvertently forget it!

➤ A 20-foot long line. You won't need this for the first week or two, but once your Golden gains confidence in his new surroundings (it happens in a heartbeat!), you'll need a reliable method of controlling him from a distance. The long line is a 20-to-30-foot fabric leash available in pet stores or pet supply catalogs (as are most of the items in this chapter); or you can make your own from a length of soft nylon or poly-rope and a clip (for his collar), both available at the hardware or discount store. I frequently use both sizes (not at the same time of course). I also use a 40-to-50-foot line in addition to the shorter one.

Collar Tab

You can make a collar tab or purchase one. This is a 6-to-10-inch length of leash or a cord with a clip at the end to attach to your puppy's collar to wear around the house. He will graduate into this short tab within a few weeks after coming home. You might as well get it now.

Head Halter

A head halter is optional equipment. In addition to the standard leash and collar, headgear worn with a leash can help control a puppy who adamantly resists a buckle collar when on leash. The Halti, the Come-Along, and the Gentle Leader-Promise Head Collar are different versions of the same type of head collar. Made from a webbed nylon material, it goes over the bridge of the nose and the leash attaches to an "O" ring under the dog's chin. It is not a muzzle, although it resembles one. It offers more control than the slip or buckle collar. You probably won't need it, but you should know they are available. We'll review them further in Chapter 14.

Bedding

You can get real crazy here. Bed choices are unlimited! Plush cushions, cedar pillows, covered foam mattresses, all with patterns and colors galore; match your dog or match your color scheme. My preference always runs to ducks and geese. After all, my dogs are working retrievers, Golden variety!

Toys and Chewies

Golden Retriever puppies are really miniature chewing machines disguised as dogs. As a breed, Goldens tend to be very oral and possess a maniacal desire to have something in their mouths. If they don't have toys to satisfy their chewing instincts, you know what will happen to your shoes and furniture.

Rubber or Nylon Chew Bones

These are great chewcifiers, and they come in shapes and sizes to fit every age and breed. When the ends get spindly, just discard them.

Sterilized Naturalized Bones

Another retriever favorite. Like rubber bones, these thick, hollow bones won't fragment or splinter. Because I live with five adult-size power-chewers, almost every room in my house is usually littered with chew toys and sterilized bones.

Woolly Toys and Braided Rope

Puppies love them, but they are for puppies only, not for people-tugging. (Tug-of-war games are definitely out of bounds, which we'll discuss further in Chapter 11.) Your pup will shake them and toss them around, so he doesn't need you in the mix.

Doggy Do's

Empty gallon milk jugs make excellent puppy toys. They bounce around easily and make lots of noise. Puppies love to bat them about with their paws and will get crazy when they play with them. Replace as needed because they'll get chewed up in a hurry.

53

The Scoop on Rawhide Chewies

Other chewies such as rawhides should be selected carefully. A rawhide chewie is fine as long as your puppy or adult dog doesn't try to swallow it whole and choke on it. (It happened to one of my older Goldens. Ask your vet!) My dogs get them only under supervision. A newer type of molded rawhide is extra hard and safe, and most dogs love it. The melting process used in creating the new ones also sterilizes the material.

Chewies to Avoid

Chew materials you might want to avoid include pressed rawhides, which are merely strips of rawhide material pressed together under pressure and have been known to produce loose stools. Some meat-flavored rawhides can stain your carpet. (I learned that one the hard way!) Pig's ears can cause upset stomachs, and cow hooves create a most unpleasant odor. We live in cattle country, and I still can't abide the smell of cow hooves in my house!

Doggy Do's

Buy only rawhide products made in the United States. In the U.S., rawhide is considered a food by-product, and the processing is government controlled. Not so in other countries where the chemical processing of rawhide materials is not regulated and the rawhide materials might have been preserved with formaldehyde, arsenic, or other toxic chemicals.

Toys Not to Buy

Avoid cutesy toys with squeakers or tiny eyes or fuzzy noses that could be chewed off and swallowed. A further word of warning about toys in general. You're bound to go overboard because they're all so doggone cute. Buy as many as your heart desires, but offer your puppy only two or three items at a time. Give him too many choices, and, just like a child, he'll get bored with all of them. Keep a couple of favorite chew toys in his crate and rotate a few others in his toy bucket. Incidentally, show your pup his toy container once or twice. That's one place he will not forget!

No shoes or socks (you know why!). Do not *ever* toss your old or discarded tennis shoes or slippers into the toy bucket. Remember that puppies can't distinguish between old and new and will eventually chew up any and every shoe in your house. No socks either, even knotted ones. They shred, and if your pup swallows one, he could end up in surgery.

Anti-Chewies

Get your chew deterrent now, before your puppy comes home and has a chance to redecorate your furniture. You can spray a product called Bitter Apple on washable surfaces like woodwork and leashes. Test it before using it on fine wood furniture. Bitter Apple cream lasts longer but is less convenient to use than the spray.

Shake, Rattle, and Redirect

Let's call this your diversion tool. Make a shaker can from an empty soda can filled with a dozen pennies. Tape the opening shut. When you shake the can, the loud rattle will startle your puppy and make him stop what he's doing. We'll talk more about the shaker can later, but you should have it at the ready before you actually need it.

Doggy Don'ts

Do not give your puppy squishy rubber toys. Although small pieces of shredded rubber toys could survive the digestive process, a whole rubber ducky would never make it through. If your pup's a bonafide chomping champ and one of his favorite toys disappears, suspect the worst and take him for a checkup.

Grooming Tools

You don't need much to start. Just a slicker brush to get your puppy used to the grooming process early on. A mild shampoo is also a good idea, just in case your puppy gets into something smelly, which is a favorite Golden trick. We'll talk about other grooming aids in Chapter 19.

Doggy Do's

Purchase an adult-size crate; your puppy will soon grow into it. A 22-inch by 36-inch wire crate or a large-size airline crate will be comfy for the average adult Golden.

A Safe House Called a Crate

Your puppy's crate is your most important puppy purchase. I won't ramble on and on here about the wonders of a crate (I do that in Chapter 9!). Suffice it to say, you need a crate. They are available in wire mesh or plastic, like the airline travel crate. Some wire crates conveniently fold up suitcase style to fit into the trunk of your car for traveling to grandma's house (or elsewhere).

My personal choice is the wire crate. I think my dogs feel less isolated and closer to their human family. Wire crates are also better ventilated, which is a bonus in warm weather. For privacy and nighty-night for puppies, I just drape a large towel or lightweight blanket over the top and sides.

Baby Gates

You'll use baby gates to confine your puppy to his playroom (usually the kitchen or utility room) and to keep him out of rooms where he could get in trouble or make mischief. Get baby gates now. You will not survive without them.

Three Golden Puppy *Ps*

Praise, Patience, and Practice: the three *Ps* of Golden puppy training. You'll need a generous supply of all three starting the moment you and your puppy leave his mom and littermates.

Praise

Goldens thrive on praise. Like candy to a baby, your puppy will respond to praise as if it were a can of Mighty Dog. It's one tool you'll use for your dog's entire life.

Patience

Stock up now before you run into puppy disasters that will test your Golden mettle.

Practice

Hang in there and keep practicing the training techniques discussed in Part 3. You might feel like 10 thumbs now, but all things Golden get easier with time. The more you practice handling your dog, training, and communicating properly, the better you'll both be down that Golden road.

The Least You Need to Know

➤ Stock up on puppy supplies before you bring your puppy home.

➤ Purchase only safe and appropriate toys.

➤ Never give your puppy shoes or socks to chew.

➤ A crate is your most important training tool.

➤ Praise, Patience, and Practice: your three Golden rules.

Chapter 8

Gilding the Home Front

In This Chapter

➤ Puppy-proof your house and garage

➤ Scoping out the landscaping

➤ Pick-up preparations

➤ Exploring his new territory

➤ Introducing another pet

➤ Puppy-proof your kids

Now that you've stocked up on Golden goodies, take a dog tour of your property. Your home, garage, and yard might be (and probably are) littered with hazards that could harm or endanger your new puppy. To make your domain pet-friendly, check out your home from your puppy's point of view.

In the House

Take the same precautions for your pup as you would for a curious child.

Move Medication Bottles and Cleaning Supplies

Keep these and similar materials out of reach and out of sight—some-place where your puppy can't find them. The sound of pills rattling in a plastic bottle can intrigue a puppy who could easily chew the bottle open.

Doggy Don'ts

Do you use dental floss? Don't toss it where your puppy can get into it. Dental floss will not digest and can become tangled in a pup's intestines. It's a surgical nightmare.

Unplug Electrical Cords

Unplug electrical cords or attach them inconspicuously to the wall or press them under baseboards. Puppies are especially attracted to loose cords. (I can't tell you how many computer or telephone cords I've replaced in my office because I trusted a rogue puppy as I worked right beside the pup!) Chewed cords are a common cause of household fires and electrical burns in canines. Think injuries and dollar signs.

Hide Away Coins, Socks, Needles, and Tinsel

Actually, beware of any miscellaneous objects small enough to pick up and chew or swallow. Any veterinarian will gladly tell you horror stories about impossible trinkets they've removed during surgery. (Dangerous, expensive, and unnecessary!) The common theme in these events is the owners never thought their puppy or dog would ingest such ridiculous objects. I know of one dog who died from swallowed twine that tangled in his intestines.

Doggy Don'ts

Do not, repeat, *do not* use roach or rodent poison or other pesticide in areas accessible to your puppy. You can't be too careful. Puppies wiggle into impossible-to-reach places.

Keep the Lid Down

Gentlemen, pay close attention here! Always keep the toilet lid down and never use toilet bowl cleaners. All puppies are born with toilet sonar and quickly discover the coldest water is in the toilet bowl. In my 30 years of 20 Golden companions, only one has never attempted to slurp from an open toilet bowl.

Hide the Trash

Kitchen, bedroom, bathroom, office, garage, the works! Most Golden puppies are natural garbage explorers and will dig out chicken bones and other rotten stuff with serious potential for choking or tearing up your dog's intestines. My first Golden was a classic garbage dog who would empty our upright kitchen trash container every time we stayed out past the curfew she imposed on us. She would poke her head under the tilt-lid and make dozens of trips in order to carry every little-bitty piece out onto the family room couch. A typical determined Golden!

Hide the Underwear, Too

Puppies, and some adult dogs, too, love to chew up and swallow socks and other clothing items with your body scent that they find lying on the floor. Most puppies are underwear aficionados and will gobble up things like jockey shorts and pantyhose, especially unlaundered ones. If you value your Calvin Kleins, stash them in the hamper after wearing.

De-Flea Da House and Da Dog

Be extra careful with flea control products on your carpet and on your dog. (More about fleas in Chapter 17.)

Bet You Didn't Know

Dogs can and do jump out of open screened windows for reasons known only to the dog. Never leave a dog or puppy where it could climb up and push through an open window. Install safety grills on house windows or open them from the top. Open car windows are also dangerous.

In the Garage

The average or typical garage is usually as dangerous as it is tempting for puppies and adult dogs.

Antifreeze Alert

Some pet owners are unaware of the dangers of antifreeze. It is bright green and has a sweet taste that attracts dogs and cats. Even a few drops can kill a large animal. Keep antifreeze containers tightly closed and out of reach and clean up spills immediately. Watch for leaks on your driveway or at the curb.

Weed Killers, Pesticides, and Herbicides

If you store these kinds of products in your garage, keep them well secured. Make sure rodent traps or poisons are completely inaccessible. A curious puppy can be amazingly creative. He can dig into it-will-never-happen places, and then chew apart and swallow last week's paint roller plus your turpentine brush.

Botanical Dangers

Many years ago, I was surprised to learn how many plants could cause anything from diarrhea to death if my Goldens ate them. Yikes! I had to do some rapid replanting in my yard and garden. Lily of the valley, oleander, rhododendron, Japanese yews, and poinsettia are just a few of more than 80 varieties of common house and yard plants that are toxic if ingested. Put house plants up high or move them where your puppy can't get into them. Be sure to do a thorough greenery check before your pup comes home.

If the worst happens and your dog or puppy chomps on some forbidden plant or flower, call your veterinarian for instant help, and then rush the animal to the clinic. If possible, take along a sample of the ingested plant. The bottom line here is to never underestimate your pet. How to recognize the signs of poisoning and emergency action is discussed in Chapter 18.

Herbicides can be toxic to your dog, and puppies are especially vulnerable. Don't spray or treat any areas where your new puppy might play.

Bet You Didn't Know

Did you know certain varieties of acorns are so toxic to dogs that just one nut can cause death within a few hours? Outdoor birdbaths are also risky. (Come to think of it, who ever heard of an indoor birdbath?) The water contaminated from bird droppings can be dangerous to fatal.

Leaving the Nest

The "when" of welcome home is as important as the "how." This is a tough time for your pup. Try thinking like a dog. He doesn't know that he's going to a new and loving home. He thinks he's leaving the only home he's ever known, not to mention saying good bye to his mom and siblings. Don't let that wagging fuzzy tail deceive you. Beneath his furry chest there beats an anxious heart that's wondering, Where's Mom?"

Try to pick up your puppy over a long weekend or during your vacation so you'll have several days to devote just to him. Arrive at the breeder's early in the day so your puppy will have more time to adjust to his new world. Bring another person; one of you will have to drive, and the other can tend the puppy. If you do this solo, put a crate or carrier in your car. Loose dogs and puppies in vehicles can cause accidents! Leave the kids at home. Sure they'll beg and cry, but their excitement will make puppy's leave-taking more difficult for him, and probably for you, too.

The Breeder's Take-Home Kit

The breeder should give you some type of puppy packet with your pup's AKC registration (that you both must sign), his pedigree, a health record of shots and wormings, and a list of instructions about food and general care.

Have your own list of prepared questions about feeding and sleeping schedules, what kind of food the pup's been eating, and how much. Bring an empty gallon jug and fill it with water from the breeder's facility. Mix that water gradually with yours at home. A change in water (such as well water to city water) can cause loose stools. Why take chances?

Travel Safeguards

Bring two large towels along. Old ones. Toss one towel in with your puppy's littermates and let them drag it around to fully impregnate it with their personal scent. That will be your puppy's security blanket in his crate at home. Use the other towel to carry the puppy in your lap. A big towel will be snugly, and—this is important—you'll have a safety net if puppy urinates or throws up during the ride. It might not happen, but you'll be sorry if you're not prepared.

If you have to travel a long way, you'll need to make a puppy potty stop. That means you'll need your pup's collar and leash or a long line to keep him safe and under control when he relieves himself.

Cool the Wild Welcome Home

Even though your puppy was (should have been) socialized with humans at his breeder's—remember, he's never been away from home—he will still be apprehensive in a new environment, and he will need your full attention. Keep the day low-key and don't invite—or allow—the neighbors or your children's friends to stop by to see the new arrival. Friends and other family members can visit in a day or two, after the puppy feels comfortable and confident in his new surroundings.

This day belongs to the pup! Let him sniff and investigate your yard and whatever rooms of the house you designate as his territory. Show him his water bowl, crate, and toy box. (Of course he'll have a toy box!)

Make sure the kids don't smother the little pup to death. Too much hands-on attention can be stressful at this tenuous time. Calm, quiet, and relaxing—those are the bywords for the first day at home.

Puppy-Proof the Kids

Surprised? Most people lump kids and puppies into one big, happy family. Not so. Child psychologists tell us that young children are not born with natural feelings of compassion or empathy toward animals, so they are often unintentionally cruel in their behavior with a pet. They don't mean it; they just don't know any better.

Teach Your Children to Respect Their Puppy

Don't take this for granted. It's up to you to teach your children and their friends that your new Golden puppy is a living being who will love them and play with them if they treat him gently and with respect. Show the kids how to properly handle the puppy; no dragging him around by the tail or carrying him by the neck, for goodness sake.

Doggy Don'ts

Never leave any child with your puppy unsupervised. If you do, you're begging for a problem. Puppy teeth are sharp, and even a playful puppy nip can easily break the skin, leaving the child frightened and resentful. The opposite is also true. Children can accidentally hurt the pup.

Teach Your Children How to Hold the Puppy

Show older children how to grasp the pup under the chest and tummy so he won't wiggle out of their arms. Toddlers and little ones should not be allowed to carry the puppy under any circumstances. They should always sit on the floor when playing with the puppy.

Let the Puppy Eat and Sleep in Peace

Children should learn not to pester the new arrival when he sleeps or eats. A puppy or adult dog that is eating might think they're going to take his food away. (It's your job to teach the puppy it's okay if humans touch his food bowl. More on that later.)

Whether he is sleeping or awake, children also have to learn to respect their puppy's space and privacy. Using a pet crate is good for child-proofing as well as housetraining and is the best way to ensure that the puppy has a place of his own to get away from the rigors of everyday life. This is not a playhouse the kids can share with him. (At least for a while. After the kids and puppy are better acquainted, they might end up together in the crate. But only after he has fully adjusted to the kids and his new dwelling.)

Dog-smart kids are less apt to become dog bite statistics, and as a bonus, they'll grow up to be best friends with your Golden.

Doggy Don'ts

Let your children know that they should never take a toy or bone from the puppy's mouth. Teaching the dog to drop it and give it willingly to you is your job.

Approach the Puppy Calmly

Instruct your children not to wave their hands or holler when they approach the puppy. If they surprise the puppy from behind or wave and jiggle, they could scare him. He might also think that they're playing and could jump on them and chase them.

Introducing a Resident Dog or Cat

If you have another dog, does he get along with other dogs or puppies? I don't mean your dad's old hunting dog, but does he like or resent strange dogs that he doesn't know? If you're not sure, find out *before you bring your puppy home* by visiting a local park or dog walk area to check out his response to other dogs. That way you won't be caught off guard if he's less than happy with his new playmate.

Remember, your old dog has squatter's rights. Try not to make him jealous by fussing over your new puppy when they're both present. Your old dog has first dibs on his own toys and treats unless or until such time as he relinquishes that privilege. To minimize his stress over a new dog in his territory, give him extra individual attention with special things he likes to do: Frisbee games, walks in the woods, or obedience routines.

Introduce the Dogs Off-Premises

If you can, arrange to introduce your pup and older dog outdoors at a local park or on other neutral ground where the older dog won't feel so territorial.

Keep the Dogs on Leash

Keep both dogs on leash so you can maintain control. Important! Keep their leashes loose so the two can sniff and feel comfortable with each other. In dog language, a tight leash could signal to the older dog that the puppy is a threat. Look for happy canine signs like play bows and tail wags, and allow them to play together while they're still on leash. There may be a few growls and protests if your adult dog feels it's necessary to pull rank, but for the most part, dogs work out their own pecking order.

Doggy Do's

When you bring together a new puppy and a resident dog, supervise their time together to prevent squabbles and make sure some minor incident doesn't annoy your older dog. This rule applies even if they seem to become friends right away. Dog fights often erupt for reasons known only to the dogs involved.

Keep the Dogs Separated at First

If your old dog and new addition don't reach an agreement that you feel comfortable with or if you think your puppy's in harm's way, do not discipline your other dog. He's only being doggy. Just keep them separated and continue this socialization process for the next few days. If your older dog continues to protest, consult your veterinarian or other behavior specialist.

Ration Playtime

After the two are well acquainted, you should limit the amount of time the two dogs spend together. Puppies will quite naturally relate best and bond to their own species. You want your Golden to consider you his leader and become a people dog. I'm sure I have convinced my own Goldens they're just canine versions of my children! As a health precaution, understand that big-dog roughhousing can injure a puppy's tender growing bones and joints, so it's best to keep wrestling and rowdy play to a minimum during those first six months of rapid growth.

Meeting the Cat

In spite of what you see in cartoons, introducing your new pup to a cat isn't all that difficult. Cats can escape to higher ground if things don't go their way. Some cats accept new puppies with aplomb while others zip off to their favorite hiding place. Our own cat thinks he's a Golden because our one-year-old (at the time) Golden adopted him and raised him as her own.

The Least You Need to Know

➤ Puppy-proof your entire premises.

➤ Check your yard for plants that are poisonous.

➤ Plan your puppy pick-up in advance.

➤ Prepare the kids as carefully as you prepare the house.

➤ Plan a controlled introduction to another dog or cat.

Chapter 9

It's a Crate Life

In This Chapter

➤ Routines are important

➤ A safe house called a crate

➤ The Ins and Outs of Housetraining

Fast-forward into puppy mode. Most Golden puppies adjust quickly to their new human family. They are happy souls by nature and will bond to anyone who dispenses love and gentle handling, and explains the rules of the new household in terms that are canine logical.

For the first two or three months, you should confine your puppy to just one or two rooms, ideally the kitchen or a room with access to an outside door. Use the baby gate so the pup is contained but won't feel alone. This will limit his space and play areas until he learns which exit to use for potty trips. It will also limit puppy accidents all over the house and your frustration over damaged furniture.

Three Squares a Day

Most puppies come equipped with tummy timers that prompt them to eat on schedule. Give him three meals a day for the first three months, and then feed him twice a day for—well—would you believe the rest of his life? Sure, lots of dogs eat only once a day. Twice-daily feeding is preferred by most breeders and professional trainers. Smaller meals are more satisfying, promote better weight control, and might prevent bloat. Plus, your dog will think it's a big deal getting that food bowl twice a day.

Feed your puppy at 6 to 7 a.m., again about noon, and dinner no later than 5 or 6 p.m. See Chapter 21 for information on puppy growth foods and why they're so important. For easier housetraining, don't feed your pup after 6 p.m. and no water after 7 p.m. A 10 p.m. trip outside should carry him through the night.

Doggy Do's

If your puppy plays hard in the evening and you think he needs a drink, offer him an ice cube to quench his thirst. Puppies love ice cubes any time.

A Room of His Own

Every puppy deserves his own private space, a place where he can escape from the hectic pace of human life. A crate is not a cage he can't get out of. He thinks it's a place where humans can't get in, his very own safe house where he feels secure. Canines are natural den creatures, an instinct passed down from their wolf ancestors. Contrary to our limited human perception, your puppy will not think he's looking at the world through a jail house window. In his dog's eye view, it's a personal haven of security.

Furniture Safeguards

The crate serves as a dual-purpose security system, providing confinement for your pup and protection for your house and furniture (think antique chair legs). With puppy safely crated in his little castle, he can't get into mischief when you leave the house, work in the yard, or clean the basement.

A Clean Dog House

Your puppy also inherited good housekeeping habits from very tidy ancestors (at least in his own den; he'll probably never learn to put his toys away). Like wolves in the wild, dogs don't like to soil their sleeping space, which is your biggest asset in teaching your pup to eliminate out-doors. It's the main ingredient in housetraining. This doesn't mean he will never soil his crate. He might. If that happens, just clean it up, be patient, and be more vigilant. It's a rare Golden that doesn't give you a clue that he has to go.

Doggy Do's

Crates are also good for puppy time-outs when your dog has to cool it for a while and for simple quiet times for both of you. A cruel prison? No. Peace of mind? You bet!

The Traveling Den

Crates also add an extra dimension of safety when traveling with your Golden. If he's safely crated, he can't leap into the front seat while you're speeding down the interstate. (You've heard the one about the motorist who told the officer he was speeding because his dog was licking his ear?) Many motels welcome crated pets, and your dog will have his own room within your room wherever you stay.

Relative Benefits

The beauty of the crate life never ends. Like when your prissy aunt comes to visit. She hates dog breath on her knee and refuses to be in the same room with your big, blond buddy. Just send him to his crate so he won't pick up negative vibes from her unfriendly attitude. Then hope she doesn't stay too long!

The Right Fit

One size fits all might work well for T-shirts, but it doesn't apply to dog crates. Your crate should be large enough for an adult Golden to lie down and turn around, but he doesn't need a dance hall. Put the crate in a people area of the house. (It makes a handy shelf for doggie stuff.) Don't leave food or water in the crate, but do provide a few safe chew toys to keep your dog occupied and happy. Leave the crate door open so your pup can come and go at will.

Doggy Do's

Cover the top and sides of your puppy's crate loosely with a large towel or blanket so he can still see out and get air. Drop the covering at night for sleeping (and for naps if he takes to howling during his mid-day crate times). It will enhance the den-like environment and signal that it's time to rest.

Place your dog's puppy towel in the crate with him or use an old bath rug or other towel. You'll have to use good judgment here. If pup chews these things up, thus rendering them useless, remove and don't replace them.

Crate Immediately

If you're lucky, your puppy learned about crate life at the breeder's (although that's not very likely). Otherwise, it's up to you. It's important to start the crating process right away. Show the pup his crate by tossing in a treat to make the den inviting and praise him when he enters on his own. You can also offer his first one or two meals in the crate (with the door open) so he'll think it's a pretty fine place. Never—this is Crate Rule #1, and it's spelled N-E-V-E-R—use the crate for punishment or crate your dog immediately after a scolding. It's okay to use the crate as a disciplinary tool. Just make sure *the dog* doesn't realize it. You want to create only pleasant and positive associations with this room.

Use a Crate Word

Pick a crate command like "kennel" (or "house"; both make sense) and use it consistently as an entry word. Toss in the pup's treat and when he enters, use the crate word. Then tell him "Good dog, kennel!" Use that phrase consistently each time you crate your dog, and he'll quickly learn it through word association.

Bet You Didn't Know

You can choose any word you like to teach a specific behavior as long as you use the same word consistently. If you said "howdy" every time you crate your Golden, he would learn to recognize that word. The words mean more to us than to the dog.

Don't crate your pup during his first day at home. Just do the treat-toss business as described earlier. Bedtime will be soon enough. It's a good idea to move the crate into your bedroom at night (actually, it's a great idea!) for the first few weeks so he won't feel left alone. Knowing you're close by will also feed the bonding process. If you're lucky and own two crates, just leave one in the bedroom all the time. Another plus: you'll hear the pup if he whimpers during the night to relieve himself.

Dim the House Lights

It's bedtime. Drop the crate curtain so the pup knows it's time for sleeping. (It's that cozy den thing again.) If he whines and you know he just pottied and doesn't have to go again, you can just wiggle your fingers in the crate to comfort him a bit. (No chewing on those fingers!) If the noise continues, just be patient that first night and ignore him. He's not resisting the crate itself. It's the first night away from mom and family, and your pup is adjusting to the controls of a new and unfamiliar environment.

Doggy Do's

Sometimes a softly ticking alarm clock, soft music, or a humming fan will soothe a restless pup. It might work for you, too, if the whimpering keeps you awake!

If the whining persists past that first night, proceed to Crate Plan B. With the crate still covered, slap the kennel sharply with your hand when the pup complains. Repeat as necessary. The noise should intimidate him to be quiet.

Crate Plan C is more extreme. Again with the crate covered, jiggle your shaker can. Repeat if necessary.

No Slumber Parties

Most properly raised Golden puppies settle quickly into their new sleeping quarters. If your pup is the exception and continues fussing night after night, just move the crate to a nearby area so you can get some sleep. Do not, as a last resort, invite him into your bed for consolation. The pup will make the natural connection that if he whines or cries, he gets released and hugged. He'll also assume that it's okay to be on your bed, which is not a good idea this early in your relationship. Bed privileges must be earned, and you have not yet taught the dog that you're the privilege-maker.

Taking this one step further, to a dog and lesser pack member, sleeping on the bed means equal. Bed sharing is a luxury he gains only with permission, and the dog earns it only by recognizing you as Leader. That goes for your kids' beds also.

I don't mean to dash your dreams of someday curling up in bed with your Golden, especially when I sleep with several of them myself. A few miles down the training road, your adult Golden might be allowed into bed with you. But that choice is best made later in the dog's life when you know whether he can handle bed sharing without becoming possessive or territorial over it. You risk a dog bite if that happens.

Crate Consistency

Establish a daily crate routine right away. Crate your puppy for one-to-two-hour intervals during the day according to his personal nap schedule. If he falls asleep under the table or curled up at your feet, just put him in his crate and close the door. If you leave the crate door open, the obvious will happen. He'll wake up, toddle out to piddle, and then hop on over to say "Hi!" A closed door will force him to let you know he has to go. At this tender age, puppies have tiny bladders they have to empty often. So don't ignore the pup's message, or he'll adjust his housekeeping habits accordingly.

Sometimes you really just need to get something done, and the crate is the answer. But don't overuse the crate! (Winter Churhill)

Create a daily crate routine so your Golden becomes crate-comfy. Keep the crate door open whenever the pup's not in it. In short order, the puppy should be curling up in there on his own for naps and quiet time. (Don't forget to close that door gently after he goes in there!) Make sure the kids don't disturb the pup's down time or reach in and pull him out. Instruct them to call him gently to come out on his own.

A Wet Crate = A Wet Pup

Accidents happen. Your puppy will wet his crate once or twice, which will be your fault. The puppy towel or an old rug or bath mat will absorb the urine and keep the pup dry and clean. It's easier to wash

Doggy Don'ts

Do not, *ever*, call your puppy to come to you and promptly send him to his crate. Puppies learn by association, and if he thinks his reward for coming to you is confinement, he might decide not to come at all. It's far better to simply carry the puppy or walk him to the crate.

the mat than bathe the pup. Newspaper will leave newsprint on a Golden's fur, and you'll have a gray-looking smelly pup. And because newspaper is associated with traditional housetraining, let's keep it out of the picture entirely. You don't want your dog to piddle on the morning paper that lies next to your easy chair.

Are Crates for Adult Dogs, Too?

You bet! I'm almost as crazy about crates as I am about Goldens, and my dogs use their crates forever. But that might not be your choice. A minimum of six months is a must; the first year is even better. Fussy housekeepers and decorator types drool over those cute doggie beds at the pet store and can't wait to get rid of their crate furniture. But if you travel or vacation with your Golden, remember those crate advantages and motel restrictions. And should any problem behavior crop up in the future, or if you have houseguests that are not comfortable with dogs, you can always return to the crate routine, and your dog won't object. So it's best to keep your adult dog conditioned to his crate.

The Least You Need To Know

➤ The crate is your puppy's safe and private place.

➤ Crates protect your house and furniture, too.

➤ Use the crate wisely and consistently.

➤ Never use the crate for punishment.

Good Housetraining Habits

Canines of all ages learn best and thrive on a routine that meets their daily needs. Puppies especially need a schedule to keep their body clocks in tip-top working order. Routines and consistency are your best tools for teaching your new Golden puppy the rules of the world outside the whelping box. Remember, he arrived with a blank slate in his head, a brain sponge just waiting to soak up information. Housetraining is his first important lesson.

Routines Build Good Housetraining Habits

Always take your puppy outside the first thing in the morning, every time he wakes up or leaves the crate, within 5 to 20 minutes after eating, and before you bed him for the night. Bladder control varies with each puppy, and he might piddle as often as every half hour that first week or two. I set my oven timer to remind me; a half hour whizzes by so fast.

Doggy Do's

Pups between seven and 12 weeks of age will need eight to ten trips outside each day. From 13 to 20 weeks of age, seven or eight trips a day for walks and elimination stops. Adult Goldens should always go outside at least four times a day.

Start teaching you pup "outside" right away. When he leaves his crate, just tell him "outside" and take him to the door. Use it every time and—Oh, Joy! Your pup will soon learn that "outside" means the door, the one he'll use to do his job. Smart owner, smart puppy, right?

This is a typical housetraining schedule for a seven-week-old puppy. As you read this, you'll realize why a puppy is a full-time commitment. Thank goodness they grow up faster than our kids!

6–7 a.m.	Puppy goes outside
	Offer food and water
	Play with puppy while you make breakfast
	Take puppy outside
	Puppy naps in his crate
10 a.m.	Puppy goes outside
	Offer water
	Play with your puppy, take a walk, play a game
	Take him outside
	Puppy naps in his crate
12–1 p.m.	Puppy goes outside
	Feed puppy, offer water
	Play with puppy inside or outside
	Take him outside
	Puppy naps in crate

3–4 p.m.	Take puppy outside
	Offer water
	Play with puppy, take a walk
	Play training session
	Take him outside
	Puppy naps in crate
5 p.m.	Puppy goes outside
	Feed puppy dinner, offer water
	Play indoors or out
	Puppy plays inside while you make supper
	Take him outside
	Puppy naps again
7–8 p.m.	Take puppy outside
	Walk or play with puppy
	Crate time again
10 p.m.	Take puppy outside
	Time for bed in crate

There's an important reason for all these puppy play periods. Before your puppy left his mom, he spent most of his day frolicking with his littermates, chasing and wrestling until they all fell asleep from pure exhaustion. What happens to all that excess energy now that the pup's home with you?

Exercise is as essential to your puppy's well being as his food and water. If he doesn't get enough, he might act hyper, refuse to calm down for his puppy training sessions, and redirect his excess energy into destructive activities like chewing up your house. After all, what's a normal pup to do?

Adopt a reasonable puppy schedule and modify it as your puppy matures. Use the activities outlined in the next chapter and invent your own to keep him properly exercised. This is a busy time for both of you. Goldens are smart pups, but they won't play *safely* without your help.

Whizzer Spots

Use the same area in your yard or other appointed spot for your puppy's outside trips. He will learn to associate the area for that purpose, and the odor from previous outings will help stimulate him to go. (Didn't you ever wonder about fire hydrants?)

Teach an Elimination Word

As with "kennel" or "house," teach your puppy an elimination command and use it every time he goes. My personal favorites are "hurry up" and "get busy." (Choose a word or phrase that you would not feel ridiculous saying in public; if you're a city dweller, you've already figured this out.) As soon as puppy squats to urinate or to move his bowels, use your chosen command (softly, or the pup will become too excited to finish the job) and offer praise. "Hurry up. Good boy, hurry up." Brief praise while going, not a lot of conversation, and not while merely squatting. (I've seen puppies simply squat and not go when they heard the magic word just to get the praise!) The dog will soon recognize the key word and understand the purpose of those little trips outside. You can praise more heartily when he's done and even give a tidbit treat once in a while.

If your puppy wants to play or visit when you take him outside for a business trip, just ignore him until he does his job. Once he's finished, praise the pup and go back inside. Reward him with his walk or other play after he has gone.

Doggy Don'ts

Don't talk to or praise your puppy before he does his business. Puppies get distracted easily: your voice, a blowing leaf, a daffodil. Start praising softly while the pup eliminates.

Use Your Three *P*s

After a week or two, you'll find that the pup might not always "go" as soon as he goes outside. There will be irresistible sights and sounds that will distract him from the job at hand. That's okay! He's just discovering the world you take for granted. Be *Patient* and enjoy the moment with him. Like children, puppies grow up all too soon!

Housetraining Togetherness

The sorry truth is you can't just pop the pup out the door to go. You must go with him on each trip to teach the word and give the praise. You also need to check the puppy's stools for signs of diarrhea, blood, or parasites. Rain, shine, or 2 a.m., you have to make sure he does his job and gets his praise.

Where's the Door?

Be sure to use the same door or exit for your dog's business trips. Within a few days, you should see him go to the door on his own.

Every dog develops his own signal system. Some whine at the door, a few might paw at it, others simply stare at the door, while some just sniff the floor in circles. At this age, one pass at the door is all you'll probably get before the pup lets it fly, so be alert! Eventually, he'll be more persistent. My own Goldens never bark to go outside. They simply come and stare at me, leave the room, and then come back again and stare.

Never Punish Mistakes

If puppy makes a mistake indoors when you're not looking or if you find it later, just forget it and keep on trying. You have to catch him *in the act* to show him that indoors is not acceptable; even seconds later is too late. Puppies—in fact, dogs of any age—cannot connect a correction with something they did a heartbeat earlier. (Burn that in your brain. That truism applies to everything a canine does throughout his lifetime, and I'll repeat it several times within this book.) *Never yell at your dog, strike him with a newspaper or your hand, and definitely do not rub his nose in his mistake.* These are pointless punishments that your puppy or adult dog will not understand at all. Rather, he will only learn to fear the newspaper or your hand. If you miss your dog's duty call, it's your mistake, not his.

When he squats indoors—or starts to squat—quickly clap your hands and use a firm "No!" or sharp "Aahh, aahh, aahh!" (no shrieking, please), and then scoop the pup up and carry him outside. The sharp sounds may even startle him to stop going. Take him out even if he doesn't go again, and offer praise for completing the job if and when he does.

Bet You Didn't Know

One survey by the National Council on Pet Population Study and Policy found that 34 percent of people who surrendered their dogs to shelters thought rubbing the animals' noses in their feces would help housetrain them. It is, in fact, disgusting and counter-productive. The reality is that only praise and reinforcing positive behavior are effective.

Odor Neutralizers

Those accident spots have to be deodorized. Goldens have a "nose brain" that can identify odors that are ages old and in amazingly tiny amounts. (Remember those fire hydrants?) First, blot up the moisture with paper toweling or an absorbent sponge designed to sop up liquids. Clean with a crystallizing carpet cleaner (dish detergents will leave soap residue that attract and hold dirt), and then generously spray with an odor neutralizer (available through pet suppliers) to remove the smell. Some owners use a four-to-one water-vinegar solution with good results. Soak the area with the odor treatment, cover with a clean, non-staining towel, and top with a heavy book for 24 hours. (Tell your friends you're teaching your puppy how to read.) Try both and see what works best for you.

Doggy Don'ts

Never use a newspaper to hit your dog and never rub his nose in his "mistakes." Instead, be mad at yourself for not being vigilant when your puppy had to go!

One Room at a Time

It's easier to teach elimination skills (sounds better than housetraining, doesn't it?) one room at a time. Goldens are pretty smart pups, but even a genius Golden won't know how to find his bathroom exit if he's upstairs or several rooms away. That's the beauty of baby gates. When a puppy owner tells me her little one always has an accident in their upstairs bedroom while she's making the kids' beds, guess what my answer is? Why is the puppy there, for heaven's sake!

Crate Alternatives

Crate use can be overdone. For the first 10 weeks of his life, never leave a pup unattended in a crate for more than two hours at a time (unless he's sleeping!) Pups up to three months, three hours. Four hours for the four and five month old, and no more than six hours for dogs six months and older. If you can't be home to tend the pup, have a relative or neighbor come in to let him out and feed him, or hire a trustworthy dog sitter.

Doggy Don'ts

Never use ammonia to clean up puppy accidents. Dog urine contains ammonia, so you'll just make the spot a good reminder to "pee here."

If a crate won't work for you at all (I can't imagine why not, but just in case), you can use an indoor exercise pen at least four feet by four feet square. Make sure it's sturdy enough to stand alone or secure it so it won't fall if the puppy jumps up on the sides. Make it large enough to allow a corner for elimination and another one for play and sleeping. Cover the floor area with newspapers. When you determine which part of the pen area the puppy has chosen to relieve himself, you can limit the papers to that corner or area. You will still need a companion to visit the pup at least once during the day.

Some owners use a backyard chain link kennel or dog run to give their Golden a change of scenery and give themselves a doggy break. These work well for short periods, but their convenience makes them easy to abuse. You can't just put your puppy or dog outside in a pen and forget about him. He will be bored and lonely, as well as untrained and wild when he's released. If you have an outdoor kennel, be sure to use it only as a supplement for brief periods of time. Quality house time is essential to your Golden puppy's mental and emotional well being.

Don't rely on those baby gates to contain the puppy if he's unsupervised for lengthy periods. Most Golden puppies master them within a week and will scale them like a mountain goat.

If you keep your puppy in his exercise pen for a significant period of time, cover part of the pen floor with newspapers. (Winter Chuchill)

Decide how you're going to handle your puppy's maximum confinement periods before you bring him home. Remember that raising a puppy without people is like raising a child in a closet. If he's merely confined without proper supervision and training, he will not learn people rules, good manners, or correct canine behavior. He won't grow up to be a Golden companion—he might end up a shelter dog.

The Least You Need to Know

➤ A crate will make your Golden feel secure.

➤ A crate will protect your household as well as your dog.

➤ Follow common sense rules of crating.

➤ Housetraining requires patience and persistence.

Part 3

Teaching Golden Behavior

By now you get the picture that your Golden puppy will take time and lots of it. This first year is the biggie, because what he learns now, especially during his critical first 16 to 20 weeks of life, will determine what kind of adult Golden you will live with for the next 10 to 13 years.

The good part is you're dealing with a blank slate for a brain (the puppy's, not yours!). At this point in his tiny life, he hasn't been on this planet long enough to learn bad habits. The tough part: now it's now up to you. Controlling your own reactions will be more difficult than controlling puppy behavior. This little pup can grow up to be the best Golden Retriever on the block, in the neighborhood—heck, even the entire state! Or, and this is a big OR, he can become the kind of dog you wish lived somewhere else. The choice today is yours.

This part of the book is about your dog's behavior: the good, the bad, and the ugly. It's also about simple puppy training exercises and the ins and outs of dog talk. You'll go through Puppy Basics 101 and learn how to be the top dog in your house without overdosing on your Prozac. By now you've guessed this is a part you don't want to miss!

Chapter 11

Socialization and Games

In This Chapter

➤ What is socialization, and why is it so important

➤ Playing puppy games

➤ Talking proper dog talk

➤ Feeding and food handling

➤ Becoming your dog's leader

The socialization referred to in this book has nothing to do with the Soviet Union or third world country politics. Socializing is a puppy's introduction to the human world. From birth to seven weeks, he's been learning proper canine behavior from his mom and littermates. Now at seven weeks, he's old enough to make the switch from dogs to humans. Years of research have shown that seven weeks is the best age for a puppy to begin forming social bonds with people. He is now emotionally mature enough to adjust to lifestyle changes and to begin learning new behaviors.

The Imprinting Period

Your puppy's brain is like a tiny sponge. Everything that happens during his first 20 weeks of life will permanently imprint on that brain. Both positive and negative experiences will have a lasting effect on everything he learns later in life and on the adult dog he becomes. *Heed this message!* The quality of the time you invest in your Golden puppy now will directly affect the quality of the adult Golden you will live with for the next 10 to 13 years! Make the most of this critical growth phase. He could become a 14-karat wonder dog, a common gold-plated canine, or end up a tarnished, garden-variety scamp.

The 8-to-10-Week Fear Period

Your puppy is especially impressionable now. This is a fragile time when object associations can leave indelible imprints. It's vital that he have only positive experiences with people, other animals, and places during this critical period.

It's equally important to *avoid* painful or scary experiences until after 11 weeks of age. That means you and your puppy are in effect grounded for the next three weeks. Just concentrate on making home a happy place.

Doggy Do's

Puppies frequently spook at some object they perceive as strange: a lawn mower, a vacuum cleaner, a large box. Don't sympathize or force the pup into a head-on confrontation. Instead, go to the object, pet it, laugh a bit, and talk happily to encourage the dog. Let him sniff and investigate it on his own.

Some situations can't be avoided, like going to the vet. But if you've chosen your vet wisely, you can turn the visit into a happy experience where the pup is praised and petted. Your vet will understand, and the two of you can happy up the exam or puppy shot with praise, laughter, and puppy treats. If instead you offer sympathy or soothing reassurance, you'll just convince the pup that things must be pretty awful, and it's okay to cower and act scared. He will respond to your reactions, so keep them upbeat and positive. See Chapter 16 for more details on vet visitation.

Building Confidence

Once he's past the fear period and your vet tells you the pup's safely immunized, commit to two or three away-from-home trips every week to expose him to new people, sounds, and smells. The more he sees of his new human world, the more confident he'll grow up to be. Start slowly with a neighbor's yard, a local grocery store, or friendly place where you can both relax and browse. Car rides are great fun. Carry him if you think strange dogs have soiled the area. I always take my own pups into my bank and post office. I don't know who enjoys it more: the pup, the bank tellers, or the postmistress!

Sightseeing Tours

Build up gradually to shopping malls and other busy places. Puppies should be exposed to all sorts of new and different situations such as stairs, elevators, different types of vehicles, people in uniform, delivery trucks—the list is endless. Visit those dog-friendly pet stores where he can charm all the customers and snag a treat. Hang out at grocery stores where he'll encounter shoppers with noisy shopping carts. On city streets, walk over the sewer grates. Stroll through the K-mart garden center, wherever you and pup can walk. You get the picture. If he's worried or shows signs of fear or apprehension, handle those situations as described earlier, be enthusiastic, but don't force it. Back off and try again later. Avoid extremes and condition him gradually to the unusual.

I'm not trying to scare you, *but* an unsocialized dog will grow up to be spooky, shy, and fearful of people, other dogs, and strange places. He'll be one unhappy pooch. The time and quality of time you spend with puppy now will directly influence the quality of your adult Golden. Never again will you have this supreme chance to mold his personality and behavior. Don't waste this precious gift.

Doggy Do's

Experienced puppy raisers set people goals to socialize their puppies. Every pup should meet 100 people in a variety of safe settings before he reaches three months of age. Socialization is the key to a confident puppy and adult.

Let's Puppy Party

Make your house an active, puppy-friendly place. If you don't have children, invite relatives or the neighbor's kids for puppy parties to play with him (supervised, of course). A quiet, placid household without noise and people, especially children, is developmentally dangerous for your puppy. He has to interact regularly and often with children of all ages, or he will be uncomfortable with them later on. That's how dog bites happen.

Equate your puppy to an infant. He should hear all the normal household noises. No sudden or unexpected moves to frighten him, but you can still clatter the pans and vacuum at a distance to condition him to the sounds of daily life and as insurance against noise sensitivity.

Doggy Do's

Your puppy also has to interact with other dogs so he learns to respect and enjoy their company. Without other canine experiences, he might grow up to be fearful or aggressive around other animals. Arrange brief, supervised play with friendly dogs once or twice a week.

To accustom him to loud noises gradually, once a day drop a heavy book on the floor in the next room while the pup's eating. Gradually move closer each time until you're across the room. If he shows fear or anxiety, move farther away until he gets used to the sound, and then move closer more slowly. He should show normal curiosity, maybe stop eating and look about. You can also substitute other similar loud noises. This is especially important if you plan to hunt with your Golden. It will condition the dog to sharp sounds so he'll be ready for the training pistol or a shotgun. Sound sensitivity will be discussed in more detail in Chapter 15.

Puppy Learning Games

Sit on the kitchen floor and toss a favorite toy for your puppy to chase and bring back. "Puppy, fetch." Your word association games start now. As he's bringing back the toy, say "Puppy, come!" When he returns with the toy, be sure to let him hold on to it for just a moment or two before you take it. There are two reasons for this: The pup will know he's being praised for bringing back the toy, he won't get the idea that you take his toy away every time he brings it back.

When he gives up the toy, tell him "Drop" and use that "Good dog" praise. If he doesn't release the toy, remove it gently from his mouth while saying "Drop." Throw the toy again with lots of happy talk and praise him as he races across the kitchen floor to take it. He's discovering that fetching is fun, and coming back to you means praise and hugs. And the pup's learning his New Word game. You've already started on "Fetch," "Come," and "Drop."

Puppy Catch

Two people sit on the floor across from each other, 10 or 15 feet apart, with one of them holding and petting the puppy. Have the other person call the puppy with a silly happy voice, "Puppy, come, puppy, puppy, puppy!" Open your arms wide when you call, and praise and hug the puppy when he comes.

You can incorporate a ball or toy into the game and toss the toy back and forth for the pup to retrieve. Let him fetch the toy, give him a treat to release it, and then toss the toy across to the other person. That person hugs and praises the puppy when he gets the toy, gives him a treat, and then tosses the toy back to person number one.

Doggy Don'ts

Never play tug-of-war with your puppy or adult Golden with his toys or any other object. Tug-of-war is a dominance game, and your dog should never enter any situation, even in play, where he is at opposition with his boss.

Pucker Up!

Kiss me on command; this is a snap to teach. (It isn't exercise, but it's something you'll both enjoy forever.) Puppies, especially Goldens, are automatic licking machines. Just tell him "Kiss, kiss, good dog, kiss!" every time he licks you. He'll be more than happy to oblige! Puppy breath doesn't last very long, so make the most of this one while you can!

Please Don't Tease

When playing with your puppy, don't do anything to confuse him or make him apprehensive. Kids often think it's fun to tease a puppy and show him a toy, and then hide it or pretend to throw it. Please don't let that happen. Explain that that will make the puppy distrustful and resentful, and he won't want to play with them.

Short and Sweet

Make sure all your play-teaching sessions are fun and successful. Keep them short so you don't tax the puppy's attention span. Take advantage of your puppy's dependence on you and his strong desire to be near you and play with you. His confidence will grow as fast as his little legs and body.

Who Chases Who

Your puppy must never discover that it's fun or okay to run away from you, indoors or out, even when you're playing. Teach him to run *after* you instead by inventing games that encourage that behavior. If he's a little slow, pretend you're racing and simply run in place or take tiny steps so he can catch you. Whoop and holler, act like an idiot, and tell him "Good dog, come!" What a great adventure to outflank your mom!

Play outdoor fun games like hide and seek. It will help teach the "Come" command as well as reinforce your protector-leadership position. Wait until he sniffs the grass or gets distracted. Then slip behind a tree where he can't see you. Peek out to see when he discovers you're gone and comes running back to find you. As soon as he gets near, come out, clap your hands happily, and call him, "Puppy, come." Squat down with arms outstretched to hug him as he races toward you. Trust me, he will come running!

On Golden Bond

Bonding is the process of becoming your puppy's Number One Priority and takes a lot of one-on-one time between just the two of you. Like children, puppies need someone to love and respect, to

Before you became your pup's nurturer, he relied on his mother for love, playtime, and his education.

learn from and depend on. Until now, that person was his birth mother. Now it's you. And you begin the day you bring your puppy home.

Tethering is an excellent way to enhance this one-on-one relationship. Put the pup on his six-foot leash and tie or clip the other end to your belt loop. The leash must be long enough for the pup to sit or lie down comfortably, but not long enough to allow him to wander several feet away from you. Make sure he's had an outside trip before you start so you won't be interrupted by an accident. (If that happens, learn from it and forget it.) And make sure the pup's been introduced to his leash as described here.

For about 15 or 20 minutes every day, tether yourself to your puppy while you go about the normal, every day business of your house: kitchen chores, making beds, whatever. I realize that "normal" covers a lot of individual ground, so just do your own thing with your puppy following you around. Chat

Doggy Do's

When your puppy runs away from you, don't run after him because he will consider that a game of chase. To trick him into coming back, kneel down on the ground and pretend you found a treasure. Talk excitedly to this invisible object, even scratch and paw at the ground. Your puppy will come over to investigate, and you can calmly snag his collar.

with him a bit and keep him happy to be with you, but no commands. Let's not confuse this time with training. If he jumps up or bites, give a swift tug downward on the leash and tell him "No!"

How to Talk to Your Puppy

What you say to your puppy is important, but just as important is how you say it.

Using Your Pup's Name

Make a point of using your dog's name only when you praise him or give him a command. If he gets praise or goodies when he hears his name, it will become a thing of value, and he'll respond quick as a wink. However, if you use the pup's name too casually or frequently in normal conversation, it will lose its impact, and the pup will soon ignore it.

Of course that's hard for you to do. You're always talking to your Golden pal, whispering sweet nothings in his ear, or bragging about him to your friends—and he can hear you use his name (just like kids, his ears are always perked!). Substitute a handful of nicknames. If you use them often enough, it will become a habit. Our 10-year-old male Golden, Apache, is known around here as the Patchman, our Patchpie, the Big Man, and a few other names that are too silly to repeat here. When I say "Apache," he knows I either want to tell him to do something or treat him. Either way, he has an "Okay, what's up, boss" attitude when he hears his name.

No-Nos about No

Another no-no involves using the correction word "no." Because you want your dog to love his name and respond to it like magic, don't connect it to negative words like "no." "No" does not mean pay attention or do something as in a command word. "No" means stop doing something now. Puppies learn by doing, so "no" is a tough word for puppies and young dogs because it doesn't tell them *what* to do.

Save "No!" for the big-time errors, like snacking in your cat's litter box or stealing food from counter tops (you can bet your boots your pup will try those things). In early puppy training, it's easier (for the dog to understand) and more positive to redirect his behavior by giving an alternate behavior you can praise. The puppy picks up a shoe to chew. Tell him "Drop" and give him a chewy toy instead. If he puts his paws up on the sofa—and you know what he's thinking now—tell him "Off!" and do the chew toy bit again.

Use Your Best Dog Voice

How you say it means as much as what you say. Give commands in a firm, low, commanding voice. What dog in his right mind would give credence to a weak and pleading voice that's whining like a littermate? This also explains why puppies don't respect a child's high-pitched, squeaky voice. It sounds just like another animal.

The reverse is also true. A deep, resounding voice (particularly a man's) can be so intimidating it prevents a happy working attitude. A "Good dog!" in a ferocious baritone will not make your dog feel happy and successful. The right inflection in your voice can set the tone for success or failure.

Always use normal volume when you give commands. Don't shout or raise your voice. If you start out loud, you'll have nowhere to go when you want to add a little oomph to your message.

Bet You Didn't Know

Whispering is a very effective way to hold your pup's attention if you start it early. Use a soft, whispery voice when you rub his tummy or pet his ears. Think of the advantages of whispered dog talk.

A New Leash on Life

Before we take a little walk on leash, answer two very simple questions.

1. Do you want a dog that runs off to visit your neighbors or other dogs?

2. Do you want a dog that refuses to come when he's outdoors, or worse, that disappears for hours at a time?

On-leash walks are the obvious solution. They also strengthen the human-animal bond and offer you and your puppy or dog improved cardiovascular fitness. Give your dog his own leash on life and don't let him run free. He won't know what he's missing, and you won't end up missing him. That said, let's teach your puppy how to enjoy these little leash excursions with you.

Doggy Don'ts

Canines do not understand human anger, and conflict within their pack or family frightens them. It doesn't matter who you're yelling at, the dog is sure you're mad at him. When parents fight, the child believes that he is somehow responsible for their anger. Your dog, too. After all, he's just a kid at heart. Make yours a happy dog house. No arguing or fighting in front of the dog. The kids will love it, too!

Introduce the leash within a few days of coming home. Just attach it to the pup's collar and let him drag it around the room or play area to get used to it. If he tries to chew the leash, as he surely will, spray the end with Bitter Apple. Toss a few toys to distract him from the trailing leash and use your best praise voice. After he knows how to sit when told, have him sit before you attach his leash. You're laying the foundation for your leadership.

Once he accepts the leash, put yourself on the other end and take your first walk together in the yard. Your goal during these outings is to have your puppy simply accept control and not resist walking when leashed. (Think ten pounds compared to 30 or 40 pounds straining at the other end!) As with all other puppy exercises, fill your pockets with puppy treats before you start. Use your happy voice for encouragement and just talk to him along the way.

Getting Used to the Leash

Restraint is a new experience for your puppy ("What's that thing pulling around my neck?"), and he might resist with every inch of his tiny puppy frame. He might freeze in his tracks, spin and whirl like a roped young calf, or tug and pull with all his might. Give the pup a moment to settle down, but don't go to him to offer reassurance, because that would reward his resistance. Instead, bend down to coax him to come to you, and when he does, of course reward him with a treat.

Now try taking a few steps with a treat lure held at your left side at nose height where the pup can see and smell it. Pat your knee and use a lot of happy talk to entice him to walk near your left knee. Walking on lead is described in greater detail in Chapter 14.

Leash walking is really incremental training. A few steps, a treat, a few more steps, another goodie. This shouldn't be a difficult process. If it becomes a daily battle, seek the help of a professional obedience instructor now or as soon as you can find a class.

Puppy Kindergarten

In times past, it was accepted that puppies didn't start obedience training until they were at least six months old. We now know a puppy's education starts the very day we bring him home. Traditional or "formal" classes may begin at six months, but early group training helps both pups and owners learn how to teach and master good behavior and prevent bad habits from running amuck. That's why positive and negative reinforcements are so important during these early months. These will be discussed in more detail in Chapter 14.

Super Puppy Classes = Super Pups

Puppy kindergarten classes such as Super Puppy can help speed up the social learning process. The age of enrollment varies with the class. Wait until the pup's 11 or 12 weeks old and has completed his first two or three sets of shots (or whatever your vet recommends). These are fun classes that will get you started on a good canine communication system. They're not structured lessons or rigid obedience. They're designed to teach your puppy *how* to learn and teach you, the owner, how to teach.

Feeding and Food Handling

Feed your puppy on a regular schedule. Free-feeding (leaving food out so that the dog can eat at will) might be more convenient, but it does not facilitate housetraining, because what goes in at odd times will come out when you least expect it. It's also harder to control the amount your puppy eats, which is important in fast-growing breeds like Goldens.

Food is also a primary reinforcer. A puppy that is dependent on you for his basic needs will be less independent and more likely to consider you his leader. If he has food available at all times, he will not think he needs you for this basic need.

Where's the Beef?

Your seven-week-old puppy will need three meals a day for a few weeks. Start feeding twice a day when he's about 11 or 12 weeks old. Meal size will vary with each pup, but the average 7-week-old Golden puppy is polishing off about ⅓ cup of dry food at each meal. Feed him dry with water available on the side. You can add a splash of water to the food once you know he's a reliable eater and his food won't get soggy sitting in his bowl for half an hour.

Bet You Didn't Know

A quality food provides the correct proportion of nutrients a growing puppy needs. Adding vitamins, especially calcium and phosphorous or other minerals, will upset that delicate balance and can actually create structural and growth problems in a pup. Do *not* add supplements to your puppy's food.

Feed your puppy in the same place every day. No distractions like kids and cats so he can concentrate on the business of eating. Allow about 20 to 30 minutes for each meal. If he doesn't finish during that time, pick up his food and offer the same amount of food at each meal; don't add the leftover kibble from the prior meal to the next.

When should you increase the pup's food allotment? When he's finishing every kibble at two out of three meals, bump up the portions just a tad. I suggest going from a level ⅓ scoop to a heaping ⅓ scoop at first, from there increase to a scant ½ cup, then a level ½ cup, a heaping cup, and up the food ladder according to your puppy's appetite. Some pups are voracious eaters and gobble up their food like it's their last meal, and others are more finicky and just seem to nibble at their food. Some puppies also go through eating spurts and will eat with more or less vigor at certain times. Not to worry. Your only real concern should be an overweight puppy. Keep your pup lean. The importance of weight control is discussed more fully in Chapter 21.

Food Training

Use your puppy's mealtime to lay the groundwork for other good behaviors. Once he's learned the "Sit" command (see Chapter 14), make him sit before he gets his food dish. At first a quickie sit, and then hold him a bit longer as he gets more proficient. Your pup will learn that all good things come from this new human leader who also gives food and hugs and kisses along with his commands.

Once a day wiggle your fingers in the pup's food pan while he eats. Occasionally remove the food mid-meal, praise him, and return his food. Occasionally stroke and pet your puppy for a moment as he eats, and then leave him alone to eat in peace. Have the children do so as well—supervised, of course. Your puppy must learn to accept your presence at the dinner table and the removal of food and other objects from his mouth. Food guarding is a common habit in dominant or fearful dogs and can lead to biting. Proper conditioning at this tender age will prevent that.

Doggy Do's

Use the take-it-and-give-it-back routine with toys as well as food, saying "Thank you" sweetly when you take them, and then returning them with "Good dog" praise. Practice this frequently because someday you may have to remove a fish hook or chicken bone from his greedy gullet. As with all training at this age, it's easier to teach a 15-pound pup that has no bad habits (yet!) than to correct possessive or aggressive behavior in a 60-plus pound adult Golden.

Continue these mini-lessons frequently throughout your Golden's lifetime. Dogs develop dominance tendencies at various stages in their lives. These measures are simple reminders of your leadership and will ward off guarding tendencies and also warn you of impending problems you might overlook.

Who's the Boss

Why is this dominance thing so important? If your dog is to grow up well behaved, he must respect you as his "pack leader." The ideal time to establish yourself in this lofty position is when the dog is young and manageable. If you wait too long, he might start thinking of himself as your leader ("Me boss-dog, you under-dog") and will consider your attempts to train him as a challenge. Once again, it's also easier to dominate 15 pounds than to wrestle with a 65-pound Golden that won't obey.

Submission Exercises

Your puppy must learn to submit to handling, including all parts of his body. This is necessary for grooming, nail trimming, ear cleaning, vet exams, and doggie times like wiping muddy paws. Start ASAP. If you wait until the pup's three or four months old and approaching adolescence, he'll be bigger, stronger-willed, and less accustomed to hands-on body games.

Hold brief daily body exams, make a game of them, but insist that he cooperate. Lay him down and grasp and rub his paws and touch between his toes. "Ooooohh, what pretty feet!" When the pup's on his back, rub his tummy and softly whisper pretty-puppy talk. He won't care what you say. It's your voice and touch that matter. I've never met a puppy that didn't love to have his tummy rubbed. My last puppy was so conditioned to our tummy sessions she instantly rolled over onto her back if I as much as whispered to her or reached down to touch her thigh!

Look in the ears and raise his lips and touch his teeth, rub his gums and tongue. Put your hand over his muzzle and gently hold it there for just a few seconds; he should not mouth your hand. Slowly run your hands along his body. Use a soft brush for a few brush strokes to create more pleasant associations. Using a brush during these exercises will also prepare the dog for longer and more detailed grooming sessions later on. If you begin these exercises early and continue them, your dog will learn to submit and even enjoy the process.

Use a soothing voice, praise him when he cooperates, and hold him firmly if him does not. A low "Eerrhh" will emulate his mother's voice and remind him to submit. Signs of submission include a limp, relaxed body posture and avoidance of eye contact. A relaxed puppy may even urinate submissively. Occasionally perform these ministrations on your lap. You can add tasty tidbits to these body sessions to make them even more pleasant for your puppy.

Start Nail Trimming Now

This is the ideal age to introduce the nail clippers, and the previously mentioned handling exercises will make nail trimming go all the more smoothly. Your dog will need those pedicures all his life, so get him used to it now before he gains another 40 pounds. Use a man's nail nipper on a very young pup and a larger canine nail clipper after the nails become more mature. Remove just the tip or the curved end of the nail. At first

Doggy Do's

Practice your "Eerrhh!" growl (away from your puppy) so you are comfortable with it. Use a softer growl for most messages and use a louder growl if he resists.

you might succeed in doing only one or two nails before you throw your hands up in despair. (A sleeping or very tired puppy is easiest to work on!) Keep at it several times a day (or week), and you'll get all four paws done sooner than later. Dog nails grow quickly and become difficult to trim if they're neglected because the quick grows too long inside the nail.

Puppy treats are excellent lures for manicures. One friend of mine has done such a good job of this with his three Goldens, that whenever they see the nail clippers in his hands, they automatically roll over onto their backs and hold their four paws in the air to get their nails done, because they know they'll get a milk bone when he's done. Now that's positive reinforcement at its finest!

Use the "puppy pin" if he refuses to cooperate. Roll the puppy onto his side and gently but firmly hold his neck and hip to prevent his getting up. Growl and hold if he resists and praise softly when he relaxes and gives in. Release him only after he's cooperated. The puppy pin shouldn't be used on sensitive puppies except for serious offenses like growling or showing teeth.

The Least You Need To Know

➤ A poorly socialized puppy will grow up fearful and unhappy.

➤ Routines are important to raising a stable puppy.

➤ Puppy games are educational and fun for both of you.

➤ Condition your puppy to being touched and handled.

➤ Use games and firm but gentle handling to teach your puppy you're the boss.

Chapter 12

Growing Up Golden

In This Chapter

➤ The power of positive reinforcement

➤ Reviewing chewing

➤ Doling out discipline

➤ Pre-adolescence

➤ Teenage rebellion

➤ Reaching emotional maturity

We humans do not naturally think in canine terms. What's clear to us is seldom clear to the dog. (I will say this often, so bear with me!) Animals enter this world as creatures of instincts and heredity, and we need to think like our dog to successfully teach him the rules of his new world. Welcome to the Idiot's Class in K-9 Communication.

The "Good Dog" Communication System

Puppies are little learning machines. Everything a puppy does or encounters teaches him something, either positive or negative. That's why early intervention and structured learning situations are so important in raising a well-adjusted dog. Goldens are bright students with a strong propensity to please, which is a plus in their education process.

Your puppy started canine grammar school the day you brought him home. ("Grammar" as in dog talk as well as early learning situations.) Just like children, puppies learn best through repetition and "Good dog!" rewards. The most successful obedience methods today rely on positive reinforcement instead of older methods such as jerking, hitting, and other forms of punishment. Your Golden must learn what's right before you can correct him for being wrong. With positive reinforcements such as praise and food rewards, correct behavior is encouraged, the dog feels good and naturally wants to repeat the behavior.

The reverse is also true. If he does something that makes him feel good, like sleeping on the sofa or snatching food from the kitchen counter, and he gets away with it, you can bet he'll repeat that misdeed, also; it's only incorrect behavior in people terms.

Doggy Don'ts

Never punish your Golden for something he did hours or even minutes earlier. Punishment must be dispensed within three to five seconds after the behavior, or your dog won't understand it. The same is true of praise.

Later As in Too Late

Dogs also learn behaviors in the present tense. Take the best (and worst!) example, piddling in the house. You have to catch your puppy in the act. Timing is so critical that even seconds later is too late. A correction after the puddle, or any other undesirable behavior, even when he's been told before, will not be understandable to the dog.

The better your timing, the clearer the message you send the dog. In some cases, you don't even have to wait for him to actually get into mischief. Let's say he lingers near the table peeking at the meat that you've set out for dinner, and you recognize that "Should I?" look. Use a sharp "Aaahh, aaahh!" to stop him in his tracks. You've just redirected his behavior without him suffering the consequences of a correction. This kind of mind-reading technique avoids the use of harsher negatives and creates a more confident attitude in your pup.

Roll Out the Reinforcements

When working with your puppy, use the same word for the same behavior every time. Add food lures and lots of "Good dog!" praise to make the action pleasant. Puppies being greedy creatures will be enticed to perform the action when they hear the word.

How you talk to your puppy or dog is as important as what you say. Your tone of voice relays your message as much as the words you use. In "doggese," a low-pitched heavy sound tells him that he's pushing things too far. A high-pitched voice means all is well; it's time to play. You won't be very convincing if you speak in a high-pitched, squeaky voice.

Master of the Scruff

In all puppies' lives there comes a time for discipline. While the terms "discipline" and "punishment" are interchangeable words, discipline sounds less harsh and more calculated, and that's the word we'll use when we devise corrections for your pup. Timing is critical when dispensing discipline. It must occur while the pup's actually performing the misdeed, and the discipline should fit the act or misbehavior.

When your pup displeased his mother weeks ago, it took but a single snarl from mom to make him sit up and take notice. As his new pack leader, you can use the same growl you used in his submission exercises as a means of correcting misbehavior. If he still persists, you can add a scruff-shake just like mom did in the whelping box.

With one hand, grasp the pup's collar and gather the scruff of his neck at his collar beneath his ear and give a little shake. We're not talking major violence here, just a quick and gentle shake. Maintain firm eye contact during this encounter and use your growl or a firm "No!" A larger puppy might require you to use both hands while grasping his scruff on each side.

Reviewing Chewing

Golden Retrievers are natural-born carriers. They love, no, they need, to have something in their mouths—anything: their toys, your shoes or socks, your hand, sticks in the yard. You can always identify a Golden Retriever's house by the huge pile of sticks stacked up at the front door! It's one hunting instinct that's great for the duck blind but means trouble in the house.

Mouthing and chewing are the most normal of Golden puppy problems. It's how curious puppies learn about their environment. It's a stress reliever. It feels good. And it's one of the hardest habits to correct.

Because Golden puppies are famous for their chewing exploits, you'll have to dig deep into your bag of Puppy Patience. It will take time to teach him what he may and may not chew or carry in his mouth. For starters, make it easier on both of you and limit what the pup has access to—no loose shoes or socks or bath towels. They all look like fair game to the puppy.

Notice what forbidden objects he takes a liking to and spray them with Bitter Apple. If he succeeds and chews a no-no, it's too late. Do *not* scold or yell at the pup. You've already lost this round. Go to the puppy, say "Drop" or "Leave it" (your choice, but stick with one), praise him for releasing it, and offer him a substitute toy.

No Bite!

Popular Golden puppy owner quote: "I don't think he'll ever stop his blankety-blank biting!"

Biting is a different war game altogether. Whenever your puppy nips or attempts to bite your hand, do not pull it away. Your puppy might then view your hand or foot as a toy or prey and start nipping even more enthusiastically. The key is to hold your hand perfectly still (grit your teeth), bend toward your puppy, and issue a single, sharp command such as "No bite!" This should startle him to stop biting or to release the pressure on your hand. Remove your hand and immediately reward him with soft praise and offer him a chew toy. If he doesn't stop instantly, use your "Eerrhh" sound and repeat "No bite." Praise softly each time the pup obeys. If he chews your hand again, just grab his collar, pull your hand backward, and repeat again. You might (will!) have to do this repeatedly for a while. Goldens are notoriously oral creatures.

Ignoring biting can also be effective because it deprives the puppy of your attention, which he dearly wants and needs. When your puppy nips your fingertips, shout "Oouuuch!" in a loud voice and immediately turn away and fold your arms. Wait just a minute, and then return to normal, but do not praise or pet the pup. Speak to him quietly but firmly. More nips, more isolation. Goldens are social butterflies, and this method can work wonders.

Using Common Dog-Sense Discipline

By now you understand that your Golden learns differently than children do, and he learns best by doing. If something pleasant or unpleasant happens during an act, he will repeat or avoid that act. That's the reinforcement we've talked about. Correcting the dog after the act will only confuse him and can even create worse behaviors. Consistency and simplicity are the keys.

Doggy Do's

You've heard this one before. Use common dog sense. The best way to keep your Golden out of the trash is to put the trash away.

Be Consistent

It's not okay to allow your Golden on the couch with you, and then scold him when he jumps up beside your visiting Pastor Brown. Rules apply all the time.

Be Clear

Use simple one or two word commands such as "Buster, sit," or "Buster, quiet." Don't nag with a long lecture the pup won't understand. ("Buster, why don't you ever sit down when I tell you to for goodness sake!")

One famous animal cartoon depicts two frames of an owner ragging on his dog. The first one, titled "What We Say To Dogs," shows the owner shaking his finger and scolding "Okay, Ginger, I've had it! You stay out of the garbage. Understand, Ginger! Stay out of the garbage

Habits are diffi-cult to break. If you don't mind having your adult Golden on your furniture, then you can give your puppy access. If you do mind, make it clear from the start.

can or else!" The second frame is titled "What They Hear" and shows the owner's words as "Blah, blah, Ginger. Blah, blah, blah, blah, blah, Ginger, blah, blah, blah, blah." One cartoon is worth a thousand words!

Offer a correction only if your dog doesn't do what he was com-manded to do. Use appropriate discipline or corrections that are not excessive and do so immediately.

Doggy Don'ts

Never strike your dog with your hand, foot, newspa-per, or other object. That could injure the dog and will lead to a fearful, cringing pet. Corrections are not random acts of violence.

Always Praise Compliance

Praise your pup as soon as he com-plies for two reasons: You want to praise the act of stopping the unde-sirable behavior, and you want him to know you are pleased that he per-formed that particular behavior.

Never call the dog to you for a cor-rection. That's the quickest way to turn "Come" into "Go away fast!" The dog will associate coming to you with the discipline and not the behavior that warranted the correction (present tense, remember?). That principle applies to baths, medicines, and crating. Coming to you should always be your Golden's favorite thing to do.

Golden Ups and Downs

All dogs, even super-dogs like Goldens, go through predictable rebellious stages on their journey from puppyhood into grown-up dog. Research on a dog's maturation process reads almost like a canine Dr. Spock. These are trying times that will add an extra dimension of challenge to your first Golden year, but forewarned is forearmed, which can make these periods less difficult and even fun.

Even though most people think of their Goldens as little kids dressed in furry coats, the fact is dogs don't think even in childlike terms, so their behavior has to be examined differently. Conclusion: if you want a well-behaved dog, you have to think like one and make sure you're always the top dog and leader of the pack.

Beyond the Backyard: Pre–Adolescence

Your puppy's three to six month pre-adolescent period is complicated (or enhanced, depending on how well you handle it!) by his gradual increase of independence and confidence. Your little pup will venture farther and farther from your side, following his nose and curiosity with grand new feelings of confidence about his human world. If you're planning to spay or neuter your Golden (and only serious breeders keep their dogs intact), do it before nine months of age, or as near that age as your vet recommends. Those disruptive hormonal swings will only add to the complications of his adolescence.

Through his first 12 weeks, it was instinctive for your puppy to stick close to his leader (you) and his den (your house). But suddenly the big, scary world isn't so scary any more and off he goes. About this time, obedience instructors often hear puppy owners complain, "My puppy was so good until this week. He never left the yard, and now I have to chase him down the street."

Your pup is entering the terrible twos of puppyhood. It's time for greater supervision, your 20- or 30-foot long line, and a basic puppy obedience class. Basic obedience is a step up from Super Puppy class.

Those first classes offered social exposure and taught your puppy how to pay attention, which was a huge step forward for a little pup. These next basic classes will teach specific exercises to help you mold and control his behavior—very important with a spunky Golden pup!

A smart owner will continue obedience training during these difficult growing-up periods. The value is in the class itself as well as the lessons learned: the multiple-dog atmosphere, assistance from an experienced instructor who will tackle your puppy's unique problems, the incentive to teach your puppy every day so you won't look like a jerk when you go to class. And there's nothing like a little group therapy to give you moral support when your puppy's antics move from normal and reasonable to you-won't-believe-what-he-did-last-night!

Puppy FRAPs

At about four or five months of age, puppies enter a period some experts call the "puppy crazies," the "zooms," or puppy "FRAPS." (Fortunately it's not contagious!) *FRAP* stands for *Frenetic Random Activity Period*, a wild time in his young life when for no apparent reason he'll run like a demon possessed, through the house and over the furniture, spin around in circles, and zoom back and forth across the yard for five or 10 minutes once or twice a day. He might even growl at imaginary beasts that exist only in his fuzzy mad-pup head.

This nutty behavior happens out of the blue, often just when your puppy starts showing encouraging little signs of maturity. I often get calls from puppy families who think their adorable puppy just popped a screw loose and that they did something to cause his absurd behavior.

Don't worry or try to discourage that behavior, as long as he isn't destructive. It might last two or three months, and the pup will outgrow it along with his puppy teeth (although some dogs never seem to totally outgrow it). My nine-year-old Golden still loves to do huge zooms around the property. It's just good old-fashioned fun to run in giant circles for old time's sake!

During this pain-in-the-ankle stage, it's often tempting to keep your puppy outdoors in the yard or in his kennel run. Not! This is a vital developmental stage, and your puppy must spend quality time with you indoors learning proper house manners and how to settle down when you insist on it. Golden puppies are such eager students at this age. Prime that learning pump when it's at its peak.

The Terrible Teens

Did you know puppies go through a teen-age puppy adolescence period during their first two years just as kids do? This stage often begins anywhere from six to nine months of age, often after that cute puppy stage, and unfortunately, just when you think his silly puppy behavior should be over. He's entering sexual maturity, and, if you have a male dog, his big-man hormones will start pumping through his puppy veins; he will discover independence, confidence, and even arrogance, all of which will probably be directed at you, the loving owner he's supposed to please.

The symptoms of adolescence can be sudden and inexplicable. Suddenly your once-adoring Golden challenges your authority (I don't want to do that today, thank you!), jumps on furniture, and forgets commands he once responded to (What—you expect me to come when you call me?). He digs, barks, jumps, nips, becomes possessive and demanding, mounts your leg, and marks his territory. (Females just stare at you, then squat and wet the rug.) The teen period can last for several months and beyond, sometimes until the dog is two years old. (Sorry, you'll just have to be more *P* for Patient!) But if you can tough it out, you'll have a wonderful companion for the next 10 or 15 years. Sound like a teenager you used to know and love?

Your Golden's needs for stimulation, companionship, and activity during his adolescence are very high, and his tolerance for boredom and inactivity are low. Now there's a golden opportunity for you! Your challenge is to channel his energies in positive directions. Use exercise and games that appeal to and tax both his mind and body, and don't forget those daily walks (or jogs if you're up to it).

Provide plenty of safe opportunities for vigorous play and exercise, and safe toys to occupy his teeth and mind. Use jogging, Frisbee-chasing, swimming, and other energetic ways to entertain your dog and wear him out. Avoid situations in which his occasional lapses in obedience could lead to disaster, such as off-leash work or play in open or unsecured areas.

The best safeguard against these adolescent problems is, of course, a good foundation in obedience to fall back on during such difficult times. Think of it as stockpiling supplies in your bomb shelter. Although most teen-dog challenges can't be avoided, with lots of *P*s (this time Patience and Persistence), they can be managed if the dog knows you're the boss before his hormones slide into overdrive. A daily sit-stay or down-stay can go a long way in controlling adolescent antics. Use those obedience tools to insist that he obey, even if he does it in slow motion. Never encourage aggressive play or behavior, and don't give the dog free run of the house when you're not home. As in all canine life stages, this too will pass.

The Next Dominance Period: 12 to 18 months

At some point during this period, your Golden will reach emotional maturity. Dogs with tendencies toward dominance will begin to assert themselves at this time, hoping to raise their status in the "pack" (your household!). This behavior usually occurs within a structure of familiar relationships and surfaces only when the dog is approaching emotional maturity.

Living with a dominant dog does not mean you must "conquer" the dog, but obedience challenges must be recognized immediately and taken seriously. Punishment or discipline is not the appropriate method of dealing with early dominance and is likely to provoke a dangerous response. You should instead demand *rigid* obedience compliance—this means "always" with no ifs or buts. If serious signs appear, like growling or baring teeth, consult a qualified behaviorist.

Bet You Didn't Know

In the past, a dog's age was multiplied by seven to calculate canine development in comparison to human age. Today, more sophisticated methods are used, incorporating factors such as size, breed, and temperament when evaluating age.

Small dogs mature more quickly than large breed dogs, which take as long as two to three years to fully mature. After age two, each year of dog life is equal to only four years of human life. Once they have reached maturity, large dogs such as Goldens age more rapidly than small ones, which is why smaller dogs tend to live longer than the big guys.

Puppy Age	*Human Age*
2 months	2–3 years
4 months	5–7 years
6 months	10–12 years
1 year	15 years
2 years	24 years
3 years	28 years
6 years	40 years
12 years	64 years

Think of your puppy as a not-quite-two-year-old. Even though some experts maintain that an adult dog can achieve the comprehension of a five-year-old child (mine and yours are much smarter than that!) living with a fully grown canine is more like living with a three-year-old who never grows up. No matter how well trained, he will always chase a squirrel into the street. He will never resist the chicken bones in your trash. You wouldn't allow your toddler outside to play unsupervised. The message here is clear.

The Least You Need to Know

➤ Use good dog sense when you discipline your Golden.

➤ Never lay a hand or a newspaper on your Golden.

➤ Goldens go through naughty growing-up stages in Year One.

➤ Golden adolescence will test your patience.

➤ Obedience training is necessary to survive adolescence.

Learning How to Lead

To be an effective Golden leader, the alpha person, or top dog, you have to act the part. (Faking it won't do; your dog is smarter than that.) Leaders do more than just give orders. Your everyday interactions can reinforce your alpha position to your dog. If you recall that what is clear to us is not always clear to the dog, you'll know the reverse is also true, that even your very subtle behaviors will be obvious to him. Your daily actions will remind your Golden—the insecure dog as well as the one that's got an eyeball on your job—that you're the Big Kahuna.

Leader of the Pack

Your Golden goal is a happy and successful life together. To that end, always remember that dogs are groupies by heredity. To feel secure, they have to understand the hierarchy of their pack. If a wolf or other pack animal doesn't know who's in charge or it senses a weak leader, it'll try to assume that position for itself because every pack requires a leader in order to survive. It's that alpha syndrome, the top dog business we talk about so much, a survival instinct that goes back to the time of Noah. Not much different than raising kids. Someone has to set the rules, or havoc reigns. Or "Havoc" runs away or maybe even bites.

Dogs are not unhappy or disgruntled with this totem pole arrangement. The truth is, they feel safe and protected knowing they have a leader who is strong, protects the pack from bad guys, and keeps the other family members in their place. And as social creatures, they are happy knowing they have pleased their leader.

Given that your Golden's pack instincts are so deep and primitive, you should have no trouble achieving leader status if you master good communication skills. Now that you understand how your dog relates to the structure of his world, you have to relay your messages in terms that are logical to him.

Doggy Do's

Practice the "Come" and "Down" commands every day by incorporating them into all your interactions with your dog. One helpful trick is to do them during television commercials. These "reminders" preserve your dog's opinion of you as the head-honcho of his pack. It is *not* mean; your dog will actually love you *more*.

Dogs like and need a strong (but gentle) leader; it defines their world and gives them parameters to follow. Leadership is the best gift you can give your dog.

Establish your leadership through positively reinforced obedience training. For the average dog owner, leadership does not come naturally. Most people have to work at it, and that frequently means training classes with an experienced instructor.

Play Aggression vs. Leadership

Golden Retrievers are such jolly fellows. So it often surprises people when their lovable furball refuses orders and starts giving them instead—sometimes with a show of teeth. "Whoops! I was just playing with my Golden, and suddenly he growled at me."

This is the real dog world. Because play and aggression seem to be opposite behaviors, dog owners are shocked when their otherwise sweet Golden gets a bit testy or threatening during playtime. (Hmmm, did he *really* mean to be so nasty? The answer is—yes!) Aggressive "play" such as wrestling or tug-of-war or rough physical play almost always escalates into the real thing (because your Golden is, after all, a dog). If I haven't made it abundantly clear, obedience training is your best insurance against such an event.

You can (and should) avoid canine "play aggression" by incorporating a few simple ground rules into your most common and everyday interactions with your Golden.

No Contact Sports

Avoid games that involve direct physical contact such as tug-of-war and wrestling, which are dominance-related activities. Don't create situations that put you at odds or in conflict with your dog. It will just confuse him and dilute the effectiveness of your training.

Doggy Don'ts

Dogs might be man's best friend, but in truth, your Golden doesn't need a buddy, so don't act like one. Your dog does need a parent (leader). All humans should be "alpha" in your dog's perception, but you have to be the boss first before he will identify other people in that role.

Call for Timeout

When playing with your dog, periodically assert control by stopping the game and commanding him into a sit-stay or down-stay. Don't be grouchy about it—make it fun. Use a pleasant, firm voice and always praise the dog for his compliance.

If your game involves a play object like a ball, tell your dog to "Give" or "Drop it." If he frequently does not sit or drop the toy, review your training methods and look carefully for other signs that he might be testing you or trying to move into a leadership position. (Understand that these are unconscious canine maneuvers. Your dog will sense your weakness, and his ancient instincts will push *him* to push *you*.)

Establish yourself as your Golden's leader. Your dog wants someone to look up to.

Kids Play, Too

Living successfully with a puppy, even a Golden one, requires a new awareness of your family dynamics. Make sure your children also observe the rules on play aggression, and be alert for signs that your puppy is testing other family members, especially the children. Unfortunately, children are often the first to confront canine play aggression because of their small size and squeaky voices and their tendency to be more physical in play. Dogs instantly recognize little people as vulnerable, and they instinctively move to dominate them.

Aggression Warning Signs

Aggression is the number one problem in canine behavior today, and, sad to say, Goldens are no exception. Your Golden must respect every family member and treat outsiders like relatives, or he will become an insurance liability and you could end up in court.

Take this quickie canine quiz to find out if you're headed in the right direction and to review the possibility that your Golden could bite you or someone else.

Bet You Didn't Know

In wild dog packs, everything happens after the leader, the alpha dog, has eaten, been there-done that, or gives permission. If you want your Golden to feel safe and secure, you have to be the alpha dog.

➤ Does your dog frequently bite or nip at hands and feet? Nip that habit in the bud fast. It won't go away by itself.

➤ Can you approach your dog or touch him when he's eating? Can you put your hand into his food dish? Does he growl or stop eating when you go near his food bowl? If he stops chewing and just stands there like a stone, he'll soon progress to growling—bet on it.

➤ Will your dog get off the furniture or bed when you request it? If he refuses, will he allow you to forcibly remove him? Does he growl or show his teeth if you try?

➤ Can you take a toy, a bone, food, or any forbidden object out of your dog's mouth without a struggle? Does he growl, curl his lips (he is *not* smiling), or snatch it up when you approach?

➤ Will your dog allow you to touch all of his body parts without a struggle? Can you hold his paws, examine his ears and teeth, check his belly and his private parts? Does he growl or show his teeth any time?

➤ Can each of your family members do all of the preceding? If you or your dog fail even one single question of this quiz, you have a serious problem that will not go away. Getting rough with your dog won't help and will only heighten his defense response and increase the aggressive behavior. If not corrected properly, it will escalate into biting situations. You need professional help now.

Bet You Didn't Know

Over 50 percent of all puppies will not be in their original homes by the end of their first year. Behavior problems are cited as the single most common reason for giving up a dog.

Reinforce Your Position As Number One

Use these symbolic (to your dog) practices every day to remind your Golden that you're the top dog in the house. Remember the big *P* in Practice, and you'll eventually do these things automatically.

Always Enter or Leave First

When you leave the house, open the yard gate or your car door, insist that your dog wait while you go in first (it's part of his obedience training anyway). That tells him that the territory belongs to you, not him.

This same principle applies indoors as well. Never step over or around your dog when you walk through a doorway or down a hall. Gently order him to move. In my own Golden family, two are rather insecure by nature and will leap up if I as much as step in their direction. My "middle-of-the-roader" will first check out what I want him to do, and my two extremely confident—and dominant—Goldens don't budge an inch unless I tell them to! Fortunately, their early in-depth training established who was top dog in this house!

Eat Your Meals First

Your dog should not eat before you do. In the wild, the alpha dog chows down first, and lesser pack members snivel in the background waiting for the leftovers. Eat your own meals before you feed your dog. If your dog's meals are scheduled around your own breakfast and supper times, be sure you feed him after you have eaten. Put him on a down-stay or in his crate. Your Golden's canine mentality will get the message. (And no begging at the table! That's also bottom-line good manners.)

Make Your Dog Earn His Meals

Require your dog to sit before delivering his food dish. Ditto for his cookies. When you give him treats, make him obey some command, "Sit" or "Down" or "Speak," before he gets a goodie. The plus here is that you're also giving him more opportunities to succeed and demonstrate what he knows, which will build his confidence and your leadership at the same time.

Once Is Enough

This last reminder is a rerun from puppy training, obedience training, and all interactions with your Golden. When you give a command, say it firmly only once and mean it. If he does not respond, help him to perform the behavior, but don't repeat the command. As insurance, never give a command you're not prepared to reinforce, and never give one if you think your dog won't or is unable to comply. It sets you both up for failure. If you're looking at chronic non-compliance, you already know what you have to work on!

Doggy Do's

Implement a 30-minute down-stay every day. All dogs should be proficient on the down command. It's one of your most important (and convenient) training tools.

The Least You Need to Know

➤ Dogs are pack animals who need a strong but gentle leader.

➤ Rough play will encourage aggressive behavior.

➤ Follow canine rules of leadership.

➤ Be alert for subtle signs of canine aggression.

Chapter 14

Puppy Basics 101

In This Chapter

➤ Positive training and positive attitudes

➤ Basic puppy obedience commands

➤ The power of a dog biscuit

➤ Obedience begins at home

➤ Your puppy's collar wardrobe

The lessons you're about to learn are bottom-line obedience. Your Golden might be ready and eager to learn, but he's still a babe and his lessons must be tailored to suit his capacity for learning at this tender age. This had better be fun for both of you, or his attitude will slide directly down the drain. Stock up now on those three *P*s of puppy training—Praise, Patience, and Practice—and you'll create lovely Golden melodies together.

You don't need much to start: a happy voice, a pocketful of goodies, a six-foot leash and a 20-foot long line. Keep a simple buckle collar on your pup. Never use chain training collars on a young dog—wait until he's four, five, or six months old (this will depend on the dog; some get bigger and stronger sooner). I'll talk about collars and advanced training at the end of this chapter, so be sure you read that far!

The Golden Rule

If there's one principle that applies to all dogs regardless of coat, color, or breed, it's this: the quality of your adult Golden is in direct proportion to the quality and amount of time you invest in training him as a pup.

Cookie Power

To treat or not to treat. That's the $64 question. There are proponents on both sides of the food fence. The most reasonable (and successful) of those suggest using treats for early puppy lessons because it produces an immediate and positive response, and then gradually weaning off the food rewards. Of course you can't use food forever. Imagine offering a tidbit to a 90-pound Rottweiler that's charging you with his pearlies bared!

Other Motivators

Food is just one of several positive motivators we use for "behavior enhancement," which is just a fancy term for obedient behavior or plain old-fashioned good manners. Eventually the trainer phases out the food in favor of other rewards like verbal praise, hands-on petting and hugs, squeaky toys, balls to chase and find. You can use all of these delightful tools to teach and stimulate your puppy as well as your adult dog. Research shows that any behavior that is rewarded will increase in frequency. So before you begin any training exercise, stockpile an arsenal of these reward systems.

The entire family should understand the basics of your puppy's education, but only one person should do the actual training exercises. Your puppy needs the consistency of one message from one messenger. Just make sure everyone in the household does nothing to conflict with what he's learning. Consistency, consistency, and more consistency.

Load Up on Puppy Treats

Begin by stuffing your pockets with tiny pieces of soft puppy treats or dried liver treats (find them at your pet store). Tiny slices of hot dogs (cheap ones) work, too, but they won't store well in the pockets of your shirts and jackets. In fact, keep treats in all of your pockets all the time. There are loads of training opportunities every day that just fall from the sky, and you have to be prepared to meet them with a goodie. (Get used to soggy dog biscuits in your laundry tub.) Keep your treats small enough that your dog won't have to stop to chew them up, yet big enough to make them tantalizing. A crunchy puppy-size milkbone easily breaks up into three tiny pieces. You don't want to offer so much food that it affects your dog's appetite or dramatically increases his food intake.

The "Come" Command

First let's review the things you should never do when you're teaching "Come" or when using that word at any time during your dog's lifetime. These are important rules, so burn them in your brain.

Doggy Do's

Always train your puppy in a confined space where he can't get away from you. Use a six-foot leash if he's easily distracted or tries to wander off.

➤ Never discipline your puppy or adult dog after he comes to you. That's the fastest way to turn "Come" into "Stay away" or "Catch me."

➤ Never call your dog to you for some unpleasantry such as bathing, giving pills, crating, or kenneling. (This does not infer that crating is negative, but it can become so if the dog ends up crated every time you call him.)

➤ Never call your puppy when he's distracted or preoccupied. Call him only when you're sure he will respond. Start indoors as your best and safest place, because there are too many fun distractions outdoors. An older, trained dog should respond to "Come" regardless of distractions.

Doggy Do's

Practice "Come" in different areas of the house and vary the rewards between hands-on praise and tidbits.

➤ Never keep repeating commands if the pup refuses. Say it only once. These are not three or four word commands. Your pup has to learn just like any smart toddler or adolescent that he must come or sit or down the first time you say the word.

Teaching "Come" starts the first day you bring your puppy home. Every time you see your puppy start to come to you, tell him "Puppy, come!" in your twinkliest happy voice. Vary your body posture at times, squat down on one knee, and open your arms wide, clap your hands, pat the front of your legs, pat the floor, and act just like an idiot every time he comes to you. Remember to praise him while he's in the process of coming, not just when he gets to you. Use the same word and tone of voice every time you call your dog.

Practice at Dinnertime

Use meal times as reinforcement sessions by calling your pup to come every time you feed him. Rattle his food pan and tell him "Come" in a happy, lively tone of voice. That tasty kibble is a great reward for coming when called.

Doggy Don'ts

Never train your puppy or adult dog when you're in a sour mood. Your Golden will sense your irritation and feel like he's displeasing you, which creates a negative attitude toward training. Keep your training sessions positive.

Add Distractions

Once your puppy is responding well (most of the time; after all, nobody's perfect!), continue to work indoors but add distractions. Wait until he's preoccupied to call him to you. If he doesn't come immediately, it's no big deal. Simply go to the pup, clap your hands to get his attention, and call him once again. Time then for a treat reward. Spend several days practicing indoors before you move outside into the yard.

The "Come" Command Outdoors

Your primary rule outdoors is to never allow your puppy to run free without a long line anywhere outside, in your yard or elsewhere, until he is completely trained and has proven himself reliable under very distracting circumstances. In most cases, that will take about a year. (If you think you've accomplished it in six months or less, you're either fooling yourself or you don't need this book!) My young Goldens usually wear a long line outdoors for their first year of life. That way I always have my "weapons" handy, and I never position myself for failure.

Use Your Long Line!

Outdoors, with your puppy on his 20-foot-long line and you on the other end, walk away and call him. Once. (One word commands, remember?) Lay on the praise as soon as he starts coming to you ("Good boy, come!") and kneel down to encourage him. Give him a food reward when he reaches you. If he hesitates when you first call him, give a firm tug on the line and run backward. No pulling or dragging him toward you. Act like a fool and use lots of happy talk while running backward and shower him with the usual praise and treat when he arrives. Follow this yard routine for about a week.

Bet You Didn't Know

Obedience training is not just for "problem dogs." It's like a "vaccine" that will prevent problem behavior before it has a chance to start. Besides, your dog will love it and will make you proud of him.

Train Away from Home

As your dog's reliability improves, gradually eliminate the food rewards (first every other time, then every third, and so on) while continuing the praise and hands-on petting each and every time he comes.

Continue this process beyond what you feel is reasonable for your puppy. History shows us that puppies *will* do the unexpected, especially at certain stages in their lives. The more conditioned your puppy is to "Come," the better he will respond when faced with irresistible temptations.

Coming *reliably* when called is the most difficult command to teach, yet it is the most important. This is one exercise you'll need to work on all of your dog's life to keep it dependable. As your dog grows older and more confident, and you detect a slower response to coming when called, give him a short reminder course for several days. It could someday save your Golden's life. Get real—do you *honestly* believe your dog will never chase that cat or rabbit across the street?

The "Sit" Command

This one's a breeze. Stand in front of your puppy and hold a bit of treat or hot dog in front of and just above his nose. Slowly move it backward (not too high) over your dog's head. As he tips backward for the treat, his rear end should slide down toward the floor into the sit position. (If he tips up off his front feet, the treat is probably too high.) As soon as the pup's behind hits the floor, tell him "Sit, good dog, sit," and dispense his treat. When you give the treat, be sure to praise profusely and pet or rub his ear with your other hand as preparation for that later time when you will wean him off the treat and onto strictly praise rewards. Now give a release word (as explained later) to let him know this "Sit" is done.

If the pup resists setting his rump down or jumps up and paws your hand, just be patient and enjoy his puppy antics. He's merely problem-solving. Your pup is one smart fella. H wants that treat, and he will soon figure out how to get it.

Take a few steps and move about, and then repeat the exercise. Your puppy should master this one by the second or third bite! Repeat about 10 times a day (or less if your dog is a fast learner). As he becomes more proficient, wait just a moment longer before you give the treat.

Once your pup's sitting reliably, give the "Sit" command from a few feet away. Make "Sit" a happy, fun command, almost like a trick.

Your Release Word

It's time to adopt a release command like "Free" or "Okay." Many professional trainers prefer "Free" because "Okay" is so commonly used in conversation. I use "Okay" because it feels more natural to me, and I've never had a problem with it. I'll use "Okay" in this book, but the choice is yours.

Use your release word to free your puppy from the sit position (or whatever stationary position you have put him in). Say it in a happy tone but not so cheery as to send your pup into a frenzy. You want to keep him in a trainable frame of mind.

You have countless opportunities to master "Sit." Make your dog sit at meal times for his food dish. Make him sit at the door when he comes in from the yard, and then give him a treat. Soon your dog will be sitting every time he comes inside. You'll love this habit when he comes in with wet or muddy paws to wipe.

Bet You Didn't Know

Your year-old Golden is still a puppy even though he looks grown up. Large breeds like Golden Retrievers are not fully mature until about two years of age. Make appropriate allowances and adjust your behavior expectations accordingly.

The "Wait" Command

This is a close relative of "Sit." Use it for going in and out of doors or cars or other openings. The dog doesn't have to sit; he just stands patiently and waits for you to proceed first, and then follows with permission. This exercise also reinforces your alpha persona, reminding him that leaders always go first.

With your dog on leash, approach any doorway in your house, from the inside going out first, and then do the reverse. Tell him to "Wait," put the palm of one hand in front of his nose, and with your other hand hold him back with the leash while you go through first. Give your release command and allow him to pass through. And of course, praise him for his expertise. Do a few run-throughs on this every day. If your dog already knows "Sit," he will understand the difference, and this one will be a snap.

The "Down" Command

"Down" is a great multi-purpose command. This is a normal extension of "Sit," but it's a bit handier because it places your dog in a position where he can just relax, maybe even take a little snooze. It also reinforces your top dog position every time you use it, which should be at least once a day. It controls your dog at home, when you eat, work at your computer, or watch TV, and when you have guests and you want him to behave. It also controls him in public places such as the vet's office, and, when necessary, puts him out of harm's way. There are dozens of reasons why "down" is another big gun in your dog talk arsenal. It's one command you'll want to work on and perfect.

Begin by placing your puppy in the sit position without using the "Sit" command. You don't want to confuse him with two commands in the same exercise. Now hold your treat lure in front of his nose and slowly lower it to the floor, pushing it away from you and toward his front feet and body. He should slide down in a backward motion to follow the treat. The moment his elbows completely touch the floor, say "Down, good dog, down" and give him the reward. Be sure to follow up with praise and petting. After the praise, tell him "Okay" to break position and give another hug. Take a few steps and begin again. As with "Sit," you might have to try this more than once or twice to master the correct maneuver. A bit of wiggling at first is normal. Just be patient and keep trying.

Once your Golden's doing the "Down" exercise without hesitation, wait a bit longer before offering the food reward. You're conditioning him to stay. Do about 10 repetitions once or twice a day. Do them in various locations around the house and add distractions once he's solid and reliable. Gradually phase out the food treats.

"Sit-Stay" and "Down-Stay" Commands

Your puppy must be proficient on each exercise before you progress to "stay." You'll need your six-foot leash, and the procedure is basically the same for both. With the dog on leash and in front of you, give the command for the desired position, "Sit" or "Down." With the dog in position, place the palm of your hand in front of his nose, and then give the "Stay" command. If he attempts to move, use a quick leash pop (upward for sitting or downward for the down) to keep him in position and say a sharp "Ah!" Wait just 10 or 20 seconds, and then release him with a soft "Okay" and a big hug. Dance a few steps together, and then settle him down for a rerun. Do five or six repetitions.

Doggy Do's

Practice "Sit-stays" and "Down-stays" after your puppy has blown off most of his energy and is ready to settle down. A fully rested, wide-awake puppy + a stay exercise = a recipe for failure.

Gradually increase the stay time in short 10-second increments. Always vary the length of time for each command, 30 seconds one time, 10 seconds the next, to keep your dog's attention peaked and to prevent him from anticipating his release. Even puppies are smart enough to figure out what you'll do next. And remember that he's just a puppy with a limited attention span and lots of energy. Long stays beyond a few minutes are not reasonable for a very young pup.

Doggy Do's

Establish gold medal goals on your puppy's obedience exercises. By the time he's six months old, he should do a 15-minute down-stay without a fuss, and twice that length of time by nine months of age.

Walking on Leash

Did you notice I didn't say "Heel?" That will come much later. "Heeling" is walking the dog in a specific position next to your body; for most people that means next to the left leg. The concept

Use a loose, slack leash when training. It's more comfortable for the dog and will produce the response you want.

of walking in a certain position is hard for a puppy to grasp. This is the canine version of you-can't-run-until-you-learn-to-walk.

By now your puppy has accepted the leash by dragging it around the house. (If not, go back to Chapter 11.) Your goal now is to teach your puppy to simply walk near you without tugging on his leash or yanking your arm out of its socket.

Design Your Walking Area

First draw a mental circle around yourself about three feet in diameter. This is your puppy's walking space. Now memorize the walking words, "This way" and "Easy." The usual "Good dog" is a given.

"Let's Go"

With your puppy at or near your left side, with his leash loose (no tight leads allowed) and held in your right hand and a yummy treat in your left hand, tell him "Let's go!" and start walking briskly around your yard or driveway. Show him the treat to get him looking at you and moving next to you. All you're looking for is *a few* good steps. As he follows and looks up—"Gee, mom, this is fun!"—praise him and give him the treat.

This leash is being held too tightly.

Keep the Pup in the Circle

If the puppy wanders ahead of you outside that invisible circle, tell him "Easy" and gently tug him back, saying "Good dog" whenever he's at your side. If he lags behind, repeat "Let's go" and gently pull him forward. If him looks away, chat sweetly to regain his attention and give a treat when he's at your side and looking at you. Be sure to praise each time he's at your side (and *only* at your side) and praise every time he looks at you.

Your second goal is to teach your pup to look at you when you walk. Most Goldens are natural "watchers" and easily tune in on this walking business.

Walk Straight Ahead

Walk in a straight line at first, turning in very wide arcs or circles with no sharp or 90-degree turns. Walk briskly for just 10 or 20 successful paces, and then stop with an "Okay" and praise the puppy big-time.

Doggy Don'ts

Obviously, don't praise when the puppy's lagging or pulling ahead on his leash. *Never* scold or nag. As with all the other exercises, we're trying to create an attitude that says "Let's do this some more!"

Make 90-Degree Turns

After a few days of walking in wide circles, add some challenge and occasionally make a corner turn and go in another direction. Give a tug if you must to get him to turn as well, saying "This way" when you turn and tug. As soon as he joins up with you (don't go too abruptly or too fast), give a treat and big-time praise.

Once he gets the hang of it, increase your walking time to no more than half-a-minute in one stretch, but you can do several stretches in one session with brief play in between. That doesn't sound like much, but count to 30 slowly. That's a long time for a puppy. Your objective is to keep his interest peaked and prevent boredom.

Progress Slowly

Don't move ahead to formal heeling until you start obedience class. Your goal for now is a pleasant (for both of you) walk together.

The "Drop" or "Give" Command

You'll have lots of opportunities to work on this one, considering how often your Golden will have something in his mouth! You laid the foundation for this command from the beginning when you played fetching games and threw toys for him to retrieve. It's important for him to believe in his heart of hearts that he *must* give you anything you ask him for. That means his toys, his food, and any object you don't want him to have, which includes things that could injure your pup or make him ill.

Use your chosen command word, and if he won't release the object willingly, press the dog's flews (remember flews from the Breed Standard?) against his teeth and gums while saying the command, remove the object from his mouth, and give him a substitute object or a treat. Be sure to praise. If he resists, you can use your growl "Eerrh!" while squeezing to add a little emphasis. If he *still* won't give it up, grab the pup's collar and deliver a scruff shake with your growl and repeat the command. This is one lesson that requires an A+. A dog who won't give up his toys or bones or food is a potential biter and will challenge you in other sinister ways as he grows into those 65 pounds of muscle. Think Hulk Hogan with sharp teeth.

Bet You Didn't Know

One more way to make your dog drop something in his mouth is to place your fingers inside either hind leg and press hard upward into its abdominal area. For reasons known only to the dog and possibly the professional retriever trainer who taught me that one, it works. You might have to practice this one a few times to find the exact spot and the amount of pressure.

The "Off" Command

Use the "Off" word to discourage jumping up. (Don't use "Down" because that will only confuse the puppy as to the meaning of that command.) Jumping is natural puppy behavior that started in the whelping box. Now it's furniture and counter tops and guests. And mom or dad when they come home.

To teach the "Off" command, put your puppy on a leash or a short cord, a line that you can tug to make your point. This allows you to demonstrate what you want without physically touching the dog. When he begins to jump, command "Off" and tug downward with the lead. When he's got all four feet planted once again, tell him to "Sit," and then praise your brilliant dog. Be alert if he thinks about trying it again. You can step on the lead just as he starts and force him to abort the jump. Praise him when he settles down.

If you have a predictable jumper, you can also use your shaker can as reinforcement. When he begins to jump, shake the can loudly behind your back and tell the dog "Off!" If that doesn't work, on the next attempt toss the can to land on the floor *near* the pup (never on him) and command "Off!" When he gets down, be sure to praise and have him sit. He has to understand getting off makes him a good dog.

If neither of these methods works, refer to the "Jumping" section in the next chapter.

The "Enough" Command

"Enough" is a handy word to let your dog know the game is over or that he has to stop doing whatever it is he's doing at that moment. It's especially useful when your dog's play becomes a bit rowdy or escalates into more than you feel up to at the moment.

You teach "Enough" simply by using the word every time you stop playing or when you end a game. Of course, use it also when the puppy gets a little out of hand. Say it in a low firm voice. If he doesn't stop his roughhousing or nonsense, you can grab his scruff and growl "Eerrhh" as a gentle reminder that you mean business. Always praise when he stops, but do so quietly so he doesn't get all revved up again.

It's always best to supplement your home obedience routine with at least one good book on obedience training. (You would not believe my library shelf of dog books!) It's impossible to cover all the bases of obedience in one chapter of a book. Several books are listed in Appendix B, you can check your local library, or ask your breeder or obedience instructor for suggestions.

In addition to these basic puppy lessons, you should by now be attending Super Puppy classes or some other class for puppies under six months old. But hear this! Don't stop there. Continue your Golden's obedience training at least through the novice level. Training promotes bonding as well as good behavior, so you'll become a better team in body and in spirit (your neighbors will be so envious of your dog's devotion *and* behavior!), and you both need the practice this early in your relationship.

When you advance to the next level of obedience, you might need to change collars to the chain or prong-type collar which are designed *for training use only*. They can be used separately or together, depending on how well you and your dog are mastering your techniques.

The Chain or "Choke" Training Collar

A chain collar must be the right type and size *and* must be put on the dog the correct way to be effective. Select a wide-link collar because the larger links are gentler on the neck and will make a clinking noise that helps communicate your commands to the dog. Find the

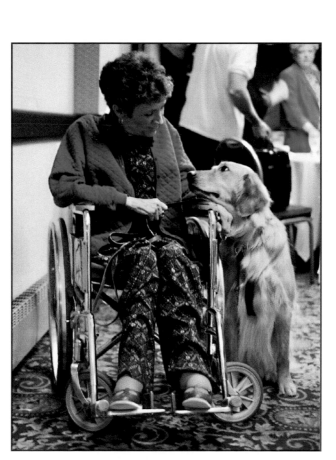

To put a training collar on, create the letter P with the chain, slide your hand through, and hold your dog's muzzle as you slide it over his head.

right size by measuring the widest part of your dog's head just in front of his ears and add two inches to that dimension. Collars are available only in even sizes, so if you measure an odd number, round up an inch.

The collar must be put on correctly to work properly. That can be tricky for the novice dog owner, so don't feel bad if you goof this up at first. My 4-H dog obedience classes learned how to put the collar on their dogs by using the letter *P* as their guideline.

Begin by dropping the chain through one of the end rings—either one will do. Hold the collar so that it forms the letter *P* around your hand or fist. Using that position, face your dog and slip the collar over your dog's head. Now clip your lead to the "active" ring, the one that allows the collar to tighten or go slack.

The secret behind the collar's use is a slack leash and the timing (as in all things canine) of the collar correction. Your leash must be loose or slack to create the snap-and-release effect that sends signals to the dog. This will take practice (what doesn't!), so use two of your Puppy *P*s (Patience and Practice) and cut yourself some slack as well.

Doggy Do's

During all this puppy training, you're going to run into roadblocks: the leash will tangle around your feet, the pup might jump and jump some more, your best efforts might be sabotaged. This is where the classroom comes in handy. A good instructor can work wonders!

Training collar choices.

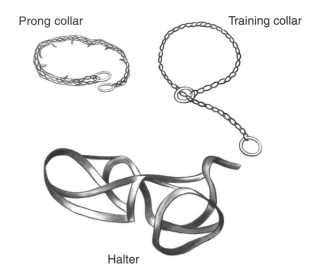

Prong collar

Training collar

Halter

When using the collar during walking or beginning heeling, follow the same principles as stated earlier. Always a slack lead (which seems to be tough to master for most novices), a snappy pop and release, and praise, praise. The leash does the correcting, and your voice says you're the good guy.

The Prong Collar

Of course this collar looks like something from a medieval torture chamber. All those nasty hooks that could dig into your poor dog's flesh. The happy truth is the prong collar is actually more humane than the chain collar, which can choke your dog to death or damage his trachea if used improperly or with a heavy hand. The prong collar is self-limiting and cannot tighten indefinitely around the neck. The prongs (which are not sharp or pointed, by the way) pinch the neck when you tug lightly on the leash, creating immediate discomfort that the dog will try hard to avoid. They are quite effective on strong and strong-willed dogs. Most prong collars are available in three sizes with the smallest at 17 inches and therefore not intended for puppy use.

I often use both collars on a dog at once, switching from one to the other as I need them. I also include the choke collar as a precaution, because I've had prong collars pop loose—not a safe event if you're walking on a busy street or if your Golden is the type who might run off.

The Head Collar

If you're appalled at the idea of a collar pinching your dog's neck or if you are physically unable, undisciplined, or too discombobulated to use a choke collar effectively, consider using a head collar. Head collars look like horse halters and lead in the same fashion that halters lead the horse (which would not respond at all to a single collar around his neck). The Halti© collar is available through pet suppliers, and the Promise© collar—used in guide and assistance dog training—can be purchased through veterinarians. Both control the dog by controlling his head and require little physical strength from the handler, which is a blessing for youngsters and small adults. The collars come with instructions on how to introduce it to the dog, how to put it on, and how to use it. All very simple for the human at the other end.

The Least You Need to Know

➤ Use treats and lots of praise when training your Golden.

➤ Always train with a positive attitude.

➤ Use your three *P*s in all your training.

➤ Train, train, and train some more.

➤ Choose the right collar for your Golden.

Chapter 15

Rebels with Paws— A Behavior Sampler

In This Chapter

➤ Chewing vs. biting

➤ Aggressive tendencies

➤ Down with jumping up

➤ Common sense solutions

➤ Are dogs really spiteful

The problem with most problem behavior is that most of it is normal canine behavior; it's *our* problem, not the dog's! Nevertheless, it's our job to reshape that behavior to acceptable human standards. That's most easily accomplished when a dog is very (as in *very*) young. Otherwise, we have a secondary problem: we're working with bad habits while we try to teach the dog. Just a minor complication.

Chewing

Golden puppies love to chew. So do adult Goldens. It's in their job description. It's a natural and healthy canine habit that goes way back to their wolf ancestors who gnawed their way around the den. Chewing on bones will satisfy your dog's emotional needs as well as certain physical needs that are important to his health. From our human perspective, it's *what* they chew on that presents a problem!

Before we get too negative, let's look at the positive side of chewing. In puppies, chewing on hard objects stimulates the growth of their adult teeth. Other dental benefits are obvious. Chewing hard bones helps scrape away the plaque that causes bad breath and serious dental problems. Just as in people, plaque can damage the gums and ultimately allow bacteria to enter the bloodstream. People use dental floss. Dogs chew bones. Simple analogy. (Forget the fact that a puppy who is chewing on a bone is not chewing on your shoe or table leg!)

My veterinarian is always amazed at the healthy condition of my Goldens' teeth and gums. The credit belongs to the vast numbers of hard bones and rubber chew toys that litter their crates, kennel runs, and my living room floor.

Knowledge Is Power

To best prevent destructive chewing, you have to understand why it happens in the first place. Dogs don't chew because it's good for their teeth. They chew because it *feels* good to chew. Chewing relieves boredom and a host of other stressors. Just like kids (and even some adults), dogs who have nothing to do get bored and eventually get into mischief. Chewing is quite simply something to do with idle time.

Bet You Didn't Know

Your dog does not do destructive things to "get even" with you. He is incapable of those human emotions. Dogs are naughty because they get lonely, tired, or bored and simply act out of canine instinct. It's up to you to teach your dog manners and make his environment canine-friendly.

Chewing is also good therapy for loneliness. Dogs that are left alone during the day can get lonely, depressed, or anxious—maybe all of those. Your Golden most likely waits all day to hear your key turn in the door, and a good bone or two helps a lonesome fellow pass the time away. No bones to chew? How about the sofa pillows or the antique butter churn?

Bet You Didn't Know

Chewing also releases pent–up energy, so dogs who don't get enough exercise will do what? Of course they will! Does your chewer get three or four brisk walks each day? Chase the Frisbee in the yard? Those activities will keep him mentally stimulated and physically too tired to chew.

Chew solutions are three-dimensional, involving the usual ounce of prevention, a dash of distraction and direction, and a dose of correction when all else fails.

Prevention

For openers, keep your people stuff out of your puppy's reach. That means no shoes or slippers on the floor, no open wastebaskets to tip over, or dish towels hanging within puppy range (think jumping puppy!). A good rule of thumb is to keep anything you value in high places—above puppy level. That will prevent him from chewing on forbidden objects and keep him focused on his puppy toys. He can't destroy what he can't sink his teeth into. Your teenagers might finally learn to pick up their expensive MJs after your puppy eats the insoles.

Doggy Do's

Give your dog a variety of chewies to satisfy his urge to chew. (Not too many, or he'll be overwhelmed and bored.) Keep two or three in his toy bucket and rotate them every few days to keep them stimulating. Add new toys occasionally; there are dozens of new-fangled canine toys that will captivate your pup!

Confinement Is Crucial

Crate your dog when you can't watch him. Despite rawhides, rubber chewies, hard bones, carrot bones, woolly toys, and squeaky toys, a puppy will still dismantle your woodwork or cabinet corners if he's left alone too long. Crating is your *guaranteed* ounce of prevention.

Distraction and Direction

When your pup decides to nibble on a no-no, remember this: he does not know better. Just remove the object from his mouth with your command word "Drop," give him an enticing, legal substitute to chew on, and praise when he takes that toy.

The Taste Monster

Don't forget your Bitter Apple. Spray (or rub the cream) on your most treasured pieces or on things your pup seems obsessed with or is dog-netically attracted to. He should lose interest if those objects always taste nasty.

The Big Three: *Ps*

Use your big *P*: Patience and more Patience. You won't cure the chewing habit overnight. Your puppy will need many, many lessons and reminders before he's fully chew-conditioned. After all, the Golden Retriever was bred to retrieve and carry something in his mouth. It's hard to battle Mother Nature; the wiser course is to work with her instead.

Doggy Do's

Reminder: If your pup refuses to release his prize, do your scruff shake thing and "Eerrhh!" and take the toy. If this refusal happens frequently, examine your relationship with the dog or pup. He's on the way to mutiny, and you need to reestablish your position as his leader.

Chew Corrections

Your puppy is persistent. He constantly chews a favored object that you can't move or hide. He ignores the Bitter Apple and keeps right on chewing. Time for a shaker can correction.

Correction is most effective when the undesirable behavior or activity (undesirable for you, not the dog!) results in something unpleasant so your puppy won't want to return to it or try again. Wait until the moment he *starts* to chew on the forbidden object. From a hidden position, immediately toss the shaker can to land directly behind the dog. He will think the sky has fallen and won't go near that place again.

Teaching Bite Inhibition

When your puppy wrestled and chewed on his littermates in play-fighting, he learned valuable lessons in communication and canine etiquette. When another puppy yelped in pain, he meant "Time out; I won't play with you any more." He learned to bite more gently, or his playmate would say "Adios!"

Your puppy's mother also taught those lessons when she snarled or nipped him when he got too rough. Now that you're walking in his mother's paw prints, you have to round out his education to include his human family. You need to teach your pup "bite inhibition" in the same way his mother did. Your puppy has to learn that human skin is just as tender as his siblings' ears and he's not allowed to hurt it. If your pup starts to mouth your hand, *do not pull your hand away*. A puppy may regard your movement as an invitation to play or chase (your hand as a prey object) and go full throttle into chewing mode on that hand. Keep your hand or foot still and give a sharp yelp of pain and a very firm "No bite!" command. (Not withdrawing your hand might be easier said than done when those little puppy teeth are sinking in.) Praise as soon as he stops biting, pet him gently, and offer him a woolly toy or other favorite chewie. Be consistent and make sure the entire family does the same. Your puppy will discover who and what he may and may not chew on.

Bet You Didn't Know

If your pup bites or tries to bite when you correct him or take his food away, his behavior is dominant-aggressive, and he's challenging your leadership. That behavior is more threatening and hints at future problems, so he must be dealt with more firmly and immediately.

Go Hide

Isolation also works well for pups who have a very social nature, which certainly includes most Golden Retrievers. When you say "No bite!" quickly fold your arms, turn away, and ignore the puppy for a minute or two. Then quietly refocus your attention on him, but without praise. Repeat the process every time he bites or nips.

Some owners use a glove to teach a puppy not to bite. With a gloved hand you can protect your hand and keep it in the pup's mouth while telling him "Easy" or "Gentle," which is a secondary "No bite" command that will allow you to put your hand in his mouth without his biting down.

Stepping Up Stopping

If your puppy fails to improve with "No bite," you'll need to take stronger action. This is one problem that *will* escalate from minor to major if you don't do your own nipping in the early stages. As soon as he bites, utter a stern growl "Eerrhh!," grab his collar, and administer a quick scruff shake while you command "No bite!" Release as soon as he stops biting and tell him quietly that he's a good pup. Your kind words are his reward. If he begins anew, repeat the correction.

By the time your puppy is three or four months old, he should have his play biting under control with perhaps just an occasional nip here and there. If the habit goes beyond that age, even a submissive dog might be tempted to take over as top dog. Now we're entering the danger zone. Reassert your authority with leadership exercises; go back to the basics of obedience training. I know you've heard it here before, but obedience is the best, non-confrontational way to remind your pup that you're the boss and master. Make him earn his meals, treats, and play activities by obeying those commands. He'll be less apt to sink his teeth into his leader's arm!

Aggression from A(ctual) to Z(ero)

Not all puppies come with the potential for aggression. But within every dog pack, there's a broad spectrum of personalities, even in a breed like the Golden Retriever that is famous for its sweetheart temperament. Learn to distinguish between proper play and signs of play aggression, discussed in Chapter 13. People often miss those signals because the behavior might look like playful or innocent exuberance. And most often the aggression doesn't become an in-your-face problem until the onset of puberty, more common in male dogs when the male hormone testosterone starts to flow. "Hey, look at me; I'm a big boy now!"

Borderline Behaviors

In addition to biting and nipping, other symbolic behaviors are definite warning signs that canine aggression lurks inside your puppy's head.

➤ *Snatching or guarding of toys.* Beware of the puppy who growls or curls a lip when you take his toys away or who snatches them up when you approach.

➤ *Refusal to let go.* Puppies or dogs who won't release their grip on toys are subtly moving toward an aggressive position.

Doggy Do's

If you see signs of aggression during play, immediately stop the game. You effectively penalize your dog or puppy by depriving him of his favorite playmate—you. Repeated displays of aggressive behavior might be evidence of a serious problem that warrants the attention of a qualified animal behaviorist.

➤ *Growling.* While some dogs are naturally vocal, there *is* a detectable difference in their message. Never underestimate growling or allow it for any reason.

➤ *Refusal to obey known commands, lie down on command, or give up a sleeping area.* Your dog is testing you. Put on his leash and start from scratch.

➤ *Stops eating when you approach his food dish.* Read the section on food guarding later in this chapter. This is a prelude to a dog bite.

➤ *Mounts your children or another family member.* Mounting is not a sexual gesture. It's an act of dominance with the dog demonstrating his alpha status. It is *not* cool to dismiss it as a macho, studly act. Tell the dog "Off!" in a stern voice and offer alternate behavior, a sit or down, and then quiet praise. Some experts suggest you distract the dog by spraying him with water or a water-vinegar mix immediately when the dog begins to mount. The key word here is *immediate*.

Getting rough with your dog or puppy won't help control or eliminate aggressive behavior. He will, in fact, only heighten his defense response and increase his aggression. *Training* is the key, and the earlier the better. The leash and collar are your best tools, but you also need a good understanding of canine psychology and some assistance from a qualified trainer who will work with you and your dog. It's not hopeless.

The Protective Mother

The one exception to most biting rules applies to dams with nursing pups. Even the sweetest bitch will protect her whelp if she perceives a threat. That threat might be unjustified, but you'll never convince her of that; these are her kids, and this is her job! Some bitches won't even allow certain family members near their babies; maybe only mom or dad can enter the whelping room or touch the puppies.

However, most Golden mothers are of the sweet variety and will tolerate visitors if their security person is there to reassure her. But watch her eyes grow wide with apprehension. She's not too happy with strangers near her pups. It's always best to keep things private for the first three or four weeks, until the dam indicates that she's ready to have company.

Aggression and Euthanasia

It is increasingly difficult to keep talking about aggression in this most lovable breed of dog. I wish it wasn't necessary, but thanks to irresponsible breeding and Golden over-population, today we see far too many Goldens that are dog bites waiting to happen. They might be aggressive due to poor socialization, traumatic training methods, or a poor genetic makeup, but whatever the reason, they are too unpredictable to be safe around people.

The real heartbreak with most aggressive Goldens is that they are sweet and loving most of the time. Then, often for no apparent reason, they bite the hand outstretched to pet them. How often doesn't matter. Even one serious bite, even for some imagined provocation, is a serious problem.

148

That single dog bite, any time or any place, can have far-reaching consequences. Whether your dog bites you, another family member, or a guest, a host of other problems might arise depending on the state and county of your residence: criminal citations, liability issues with insurance companies, civil suits, small to enormous expenses from emergency room fees to plastic surgery, and the ultimate heartbreak, euthanasia.

Bet You Didn't Know

In adult dogs, aggression is the most serious behavior problem encountered by veterinarians and dog trainers. According to the Humane Society of the United States, more than one million dog bites are reported annually. Even worse, it's estimated that five times that number go unreported every year.

Be honest about this. If your dog is a threat to strangers or to your own family, you must take every step necessary to rehabilitate the animal. You'll need help from a professional. You also must be realistic and accept the fact that some Goldens cannot be rehabbed and should be euthanized. If you love your Golden, help him across to the Rainbow Bridge before he hurts someone else and you have to deal with more regrets.

Jumping

Jumping up is perfectly natural canine behavior. Your puppy has been doing it ever since he was about three weeks old. He jumped up to lick his mother's muzzle and started pouncing on his littermates before he left the whelping box, then progressed to jumping on gates, barriers, or whatever else stood between him and the person on the other side. What's more, he was such a cutie he was rewarded for that behavior with a scratch behind the ear or even a healthy scoop into loving arms. Talk about reinforcement!

The usual prevent-it-before-it-becomes-a-habit theory is almost hopeless under these circumstances, considering your puppy's early conditioning that jumping is fun and produces positive results. You are faced with reconditioning and teaching alternate behavior. That's not an impossible task, but it will take time, patience, and the cooperation of your family (especially the kids) and your friends. If your friends refuse to cooperate, don't invite them over until your dog is two years old and fully trained. Consistency is a key element in correcting jumping. You cannot allow it one day, and then correct it the next. Neither can anyone else. *Never* means *never*. Everyone means any human being who meets or sees your dog.

Doggy Don'ts

Don't make jumping joyous. First understand what you should *not* do when your dog or puppy jumps. Your worst response is to pet or hug him. That will only encourage him to jump some more! He's already revved his motor because you came home from the movies or someone came to visit.

Jumping Corrections

The two most commonly used and successful jump corrections involve a leash or a spritzer bottle. The leash might be more convenient because it's easier to keep a short check cord on the dog's collar than to carry a spray bottle around on your belt. There are other methods, but I'll describe these first.

Use the Leash

Start with a full leash on your puppy. When he starts to jump up on you or someone else, grasp the leash about two feet from the collar, give a quick snap downward and sideways (so you won't injure his young neck and throat), and command "Off" in a firm voice. Don't use the word "Down," so he doesn't confuse that word with the obedience exercise. As soon as he has all four feet back on the ground, quietly (*quietly* is a key word here; he's already too exuberant!) tell him what a good dog he is. If he knows the "Sit" command, you can then immediately tell him to "Sit." *Now* he has done something you can praise him for. Use soft, easy praise so the dog doesn't get excited and jump up again.

The best way to address behaviors you don't want to encourage is to prevent them to begin with. How to solve this problem is pretty obvious.

Spray Bottle

The spritzer technique also works for some dogs (and people). Fill a spray bottle with water. When your puppy starts to jump, tell him "Off" and squirt him with a spritz of water. Now turn your back and leave the room for a minute or so. Do not praise the puppy when you return.

Try this for several days until the puppy shows some control in jumping situations. Once he resists jumping, skip the spray and add the "Sit" command when you think he's tempted to jump up. Follow with the "Sit" technique described in the leash paragraph earlier.

Turn the Other Cheek

Isolation sometimes works well without the water spritz. When the puppy jumps or starts to jump on you, say "Off!" and quickly turn away with your arms folded in front of you. Keep turned from the dog and refuse to look at him for a few minutes. No praise afterward; just resume your normal behavior. The puppy should discover that every time he jumps, he is deprived of your companionship, which is what the jumping was all about in the first place.

Shaker Cans

Some owners have success using their shaker can as a jump deterrent. Keep one by the front door and rattle it loudly as soon as he begins to jump. Say "Off!," praise him when all four feet hit the ground, and give a (by now you're way ahead of me!) "Sit" command.

Let's Shake Hands

There's yet one more jumping correction if you're caught off guard outdoors and don't have a leash, spritzer bottle, or shaker can handy. When the dog jumps up and you suddenly realize you have no counter-conditioner available, quickly grasp his paws and hold them in the air. Don't squeeze; just grip them firmly, not painfully, and without moving or uttering a word. Eventually he'll wonder how to get out of this predicament, and he'll start to whine or struggle. Wait a few more seconds, and then let go and order the dog to "Sit" if he has learned that command.

How *Not* to Correct Jumping

Do not bang the dog in the chest with your knee. That could harm your puppy, and he will only learn to be afraid of you. Some dogs also view the knee as a game and become even more excited, which is exactly what you're trying to avoid.

Do not step on his back toes with your foot. It's a clumsy maneuver that could injure the dog's feet if you press on them, and might hurt both of you if you fail and fall down as some folks do. And he will only learn to shy away from you rather than *not* jump up.

I suggest that you use whatever you find works best as long as it doesn't harm, confuse, or scare the dog.

Jumping Corrections for Kids

This is seldom easy. Training kids to not encourage jumping up is usually like putting water in a sieve. Little folks with their quick movements and squeaky voices stir up memories of the whelping box, and your puppy will instinctively chase or jump on children. In many families, there's usually one child a dog senses he can dominate, and that one becomes his equal, like his littermate. Those situations always call for parental intervention.

Set aside some time during the puppy's play period to work with the child and puppy together to teach him not to jump on his favorite target. With your puppy on a leash or long line and one end attached to your waist or belt to make sure you have control, have the child move about nearby. When your puppy starts to jump or give chase, tug quickly on the leash and speak your firmest "Off!" then "Sit," and then praise. If he repeats the jump a second time, follow the "Off'" with a brief but snappy scruff shake and an "Eerrhh!" Release and praise.

You'll need to repeat this exercise several days in a row (more than once a day if possible), and then once a week for a while until you get a solid take. Fortunately, the kids grow taller and bigger and less enticing for the pup. But do you want to wait that long?

Kid-proofing takes time, but in the long run you will *save* precious time extricating your child from puppy misbehavior.

Friends, Romans, *Everyone*

Friend-proofing can be sticky. You'll have to be assertive and request that your friends not encourage jumping and allow you to use your jumping corrections. Tell them to think long-term and 65 pounds compared to this 15-pound ball of fluff. Remind them of that future day when the dog will have muddy paws, and they'll be wearing white designer slacks.

Doggy Do's

Hint: Keep a leash and a spritzer bottle inside your front door for those unexpected times when someone visits.

Digging

Some dogs dig; others never do. Digging holes is a naturally doggy thing to do, but it can drive an avid gardener to his compost pile. If your yard looks like a mini-minefield thanks to your digging Golden, try to identify the reason for this behavior before you despair and pour a concrete lawn.

Digging is most often the result of boredom. You own this Golden for companionship. Companions forge their bond through regular play and exercise—together. Without that kind of stimulation, your Golden might turn to digging or other creative forms of destructive behavior to alleviate his boredom or malaise.

If you think the dog is hot and is building a cool, damp earth spa to lay in during summer weather, set out a small child's swimming pool or move him to a cooler location indoors. Of course, you must do the obvious and make sure the dog has access to shade and cool drinking water throughout the day.

Are the dog's nails trimmed and short? Long, unclipped nails automatically lend themselves to soil-tilling habits. If you don't clip his nails, ask your vet to show you how or have a groomer do it for you.

You can booby trap your dog's hole with buried chicken wire, hot pepper, even the dog's own feces, so he will scratch into them and become disgusted with his digging site. Another remedy: from one of your secret hiding places, (by now you should have several), try tossing a shaker can to land near him as he digs.

A Hole of One's Own

You can also give your dog his own digging spot. When you see him digging, take him to his appointed place. Some dogs love it, especially if the hole is already started and the earth is soft. Puppies are more prone to dig, but take heart! They usually outgrow the habit.

As with most things doggy, the best solution is prevention. If you can't supervise your dog, keep him indoors and out of holes and pool halls. If your dog could talk, he would tell you that digging is a natural and self-rewarding behavior and only *you* find it offensive.

Running Away

Unfortunately, there are no quick fixes for the dog that bolts, whether it's through the open front door or from the yard into the street. I could write volumes on boundary training outdoors and proofing your dog to come, sit, stay, and down under the most attractive of distractions. But the fact remains: your wonderful

Golden buddy is still a dog. He's a creature of unpredictable instincts that can and usually will surface when you least expect them.

Boundary training will not contain your dog forever. The only guarantee in dog life is that your perfectly behaved six- or eight-year-old dog *will* one day chase a single rabbit, pursue a wayward squirrel, or dash through the open door because he sees something only he finds incredibly tempting. When that happens, there are no second chances. Ask anyone who has ever lost their very beloved and "obedient" Golden under a set of truck tires.

Eating Feces

This "unmentionable" is a common problem that occurs at some time during nearly every dog's life. It's called *coprophagia* and although it's disgusting, it's rarely harmful and it happens in the best of canine families. In the wild, canine scavengers scrounge for their meals and find partially digested food in another animal's feces, yucky as that might be to us.

I'll offer you a few things that have worked for some dogs with that tendency. The first, easiest, and most obvious is to pick up the stools at

Doggy Do's

Keep your dog on a leash. Fence your yard and lock the gate. Build a dog run or install invisible fencing. Do not take chances and don't trust your five-year-old kid to walk your dog. This bundle of gold is a precious resource you can't afford to risk.

once. He can't eat what isn't there, and he will probably outgrow the habit. You can also mine the stools with a few drops of Tabasco when the dog isn't looking. Once he eats it, he should decide that it's pretty awful stuff. Try adding a bit of meat tenderizer to his food, which is supposed to reduce fecal palatability. Two commercially available product called For-Bid and Distaste work reasonably well for many dogs.

The up side is that puppies who eat their stools seldom continue this practice into adulthood. The flip side is that if they eat another dog's stools, they could become infested with whatever parasites that animal might harbor. So it's worth the effort to eradicate the habit.

The Classic "Guilty" Look

"He's just plain spiteful. He knew what he did was wrong." You've heard that one before. Maybe you've even said it yourself. The dog knew he was naughty because he had this guilty look on his muzzle every time his owner found a pile of feces or shredded Kleenex on the floor. Naturally, the owner snarled at the dog, maybe even dragged him over to the crime scene to remind him just how bad he was. And, naturally, the dog cringed and tucked his tail. His owner is enraged, but intelligent people like you understand that the dog's reacting to the anger, not the mess in the living room.

Dogs learn by repetition. Hereafter whenever the dog sees the shredded tissue in the same room with his owner, he knows the boss is going to go bonkers. He will never understand it's because he tore up those tissues a few hours earlier. This is simply another case of what's obvious to us is not clear to the dog.

What should also be perfectly clear is that if you remove the tissue source, you will remove the problem. Move the wastebasket, for goodness sake! These are grin-and-bear-it times. If you're not at home to supervise your dog, you can't discipline him for his mischief in your absence, but you *can* prevent future accidents from happening. Remove temptation, take the dog for an extra walk, and crate him when you're gone.

Food Guarding

Food guarding doesn't happen overnight. Your puppy will give you warning signs, and if you ignore them, he will get wolflike and protect his toys as well as his food. Look back in time. Does he occasionally stop chewing when you approach while he's eating, maybe just keep his head tucked in the bowl, and kind of freeze in place without munching? Does he ever, even once, grumble at the kids or you during his meal? That's a growl, plain and simple, and it's not necessary or acceptable.

Condition your puppy from day one, and this will never happen. Reread the chapter on your puppy's introduction to the human world and the discussion on handling his food and food dish when he eats.

Reclaiming Authority

Reprogram the dog's mealtime. Start by placing his food ⌐ open area. Eating in a corner will encourage him to expect priva⌐ and exert control over his personal space when he's eating.

Divide his kibble into small amounts so that you have to pick up the bowl to refill it a few times during each meal. After a few days, leave his food bowl down and squat down to add the small portions as he finishes each one. Occasionally, toss a goodie like a cube of cheese or baloney into the bowl while he eats.

When food guarding occurs, you can bet your food budget there are other problems in your dog relationship. Somewhere along the chow line, he has acquired the upper paw. He's probably also possessive of his toys or a favorite bone, and you just haven't noticed. Go back to the basics (that's obedience training, but you already knew that) to remind him you're the one who buys the dog food and the toys. Make him sit before he gets his food pan; put the dog on a down-stay for a hour once a day. No on-demand petting or treating. As with meals, he has to sit or down submissively before he gets his TLC. Don't worry; he won't mind that. Your dog needs a leader, not a lover.

Separation Anxiety

In a few words, you can avoid the demon of separation distress and anxiety. If you condition your puppy to being left alone in his crate (briefly) from his first days at home, he will automatically learn that your comings and goings are part of his everyday routine, and he won't become upset by that.

Conditioning and Precautions

Always keep your departures and returns low-key. Don't shower your dog with big displays of attention or affectionate good-byes when you leave the house or come back home. You don't want to create separation distress where none exists! Bear in mind that the dog is a pack animal and, like Adam, was not meant to be alone.

Start by teaching him to stay in his crate while you're at home, working in another room or in the yard. If he's a happy crate pup (and he should be), he will just curl up in his den and take a nap. Vary the length of time that you're away—10 minutes one day, a half-hour the next.

If you feel (or hear!) that he becomes agitated as soon as you leave, do lots of practice runs. Calmly put on your coat, pick up your car keys, step out the door and close it, come immediately back in, release him from his crate, and give a "Down" command. When he's down and quiet, calmly praise. Do this for a week or two, and gradually increase and vary the time you stand outside the door. Do *not* offer sympathy or sweet talk like "Oooohh, did my big baby miss her momma?" On the other hand, never punish your dog for his anxiety. Both techniques will surely make it worse.

Exercise, the great canine cure-all, also helps. A dog that is tired mentally and physically is more likely to fall asleep once he accepts your absence. An exercised dog is more content; he's had his bonding time and feels secure again.

Doggy Do's

To make your departure less stressful for your Golden, try a little peanut butter. Spread a small dab on a rubber chew toy or press it inside a sterilized hard bone and give it to the dog just before you leave the house. It will create a pleasant association with your leaving and will keep him happily occupied while you're gone.

Tidbits and Treats

If your Golden is a chow hound, try leaving him a "sustained-release" food device. Stuff a Kong toy or sterilized marrow bone with a blob of peanut butter or squeeze cheese. He will spend hours trying to lick it out. One commercial gadget called the Buster Cube holds food kibbles or freeze-dried liver. The multi-chambered cube releases food particles one or two pieces at a time as the dog pushes or rolls it with his nose or paw.

Lassie Reruns

Of course, there's always the obvious: leave a radio or television on during your absence, and a light on if you're out after dark. It will make missing you a little easier.

Counter Exploring

Once a puppy has a little leg underneath him, he might decide to investigate the world above eye level. That world could include your counters and your tabletops. And those places might include your dinner. Start preventive measures before he learns about the joys of counter theft.

Keepin' Off the Counters

Start with a simple setup. Place a tempting plate of meat or other tantalizing edible near the counter's edge. Put on your psychic hat and wait. When the pup strolls by, he'll tilt up his head in air-scent mode and sniff his way toward the bounty on the counter. You're reading his mind! Now give him a stern "Aaahhh, aaahhh!" and then watch him slink away. Use your psychic powers often while he's still young and impressionable so he will grow up to believe you're always one step in front of him.

Beyond Thievery

If your dog succeeds in stealing tonight's main course or you discover he's been inspecting counters, you'll have to set him up for the big self-correction. Make three shaker cans (as described in Chapter 7) and fasten them together with a length of thread taped to the tops. Tie another thread from the cans to a food lure that is secured to the counter so it won't fall down with the cans. Place the entire booby trap where the dog can grab or steal it, and then hide from view. A clattering pile of shaker cans should convince him that the sky has fallen, and the dog won't go there or try it again. Be quick to pick up any edible food before he can recover from the shock.

Furniture Rules

If you want to keep dog hair off your dark wool slacks and out of your face while you sleep, decide right now not to allow your Golden puppy on your bed or furniture. It only takes one time, one tiny cuddle on the couch or easy chair, and he will believe it's okay all the time. After all, that's how a dog's mind works.

Use Your Collar Tab

If at some point you notice your puppy is tempted to jump up on the sofa, whether to join you, Pastor Brown, or maybe just take a little snooze, keep his leash or short check cord on him in the house. Walk beside that piece of furniture and when he makes his move, snap his lead and tell him "No!" Repeat several times to reinforce your message.

If you're desperate to sit and snuggle with your puppy while you read or watch TV, slide down onto the floor beside the couch and enjoy those moments at *his* level.

Your Dog's Recliner

If you choose to give your Golden his own chair or piece of furniture like some dog folks I know, invite him up. He will remember! If he attempts to climb on something else, snap him off with his leash and take him over to his chair and show him "Up." Make sure the chair is big enough for both of you!

Thunderphobia

If your dog is afraid of loud noises such as thunderstorms or firecrackers, you can try some counter-conditioning to help him overcome those fears. The protocol is a long and delicate process, but worth the effort because of the potential danger to the dog (running away during a storm) and destruction of property during his fright.

Make a recording of the offending noise. Then expose him to the noise by playing it softly at a low level that won't upset him. If the dog appears tense or uneasy, reduce the sound level until he is calm and relaxed. Conduct the sessions during mealtimes and petting sessions to create a positive association. Begin with short sessions but increase the volume during each one over whatever period of time he takes to relax the dog with each increased noise volume. Continue very gradually until he shows no fear of the noise.

Drugs such as Valium and other tranquilizers do not provide a long-term solution to the problem. Sound sensitivity usually gets worse with age, so treat the signs as soon as they appear.

Electronic Training

The best advice on using an electronic collar to train your dog is—*don't*. Electronic collars are dangerous training tools that can do far more harm than good. This type of equipment is not a magic bullet that will solve your training problems or make your dog come, sit, or stay put.

Doggy Don'ts

Never coddle your dog when he shows signs of fear because that will only encourage the behavior. You should also provide a safe, enclosed place such as a crate with a blanket over it, but don't lock him in or confine him in any way. He needs to retain a sense that he can escape if he so chooses.

Before a dog can be trained with an electronic collar, the animal must have a complete understanding of the exercise or command, which means he has to be taught before it is reinforced (or command-conditioned) with the collar. If you're unable to teach your dog how to behave by using traditional training methods, you won't become a better teacher nor will your dog learn his lessons just because he's wearing an electronic device around his neck.

Additionally, the timing of any collar reinforcement is extremely critical, and it's far too easy to teach *incorrectly*. I've personally seen too many fine dogs ruined because their owners used electronic collars stupidly or with a vengeance.

It's also too convenient to use the collar for what you perceive is disobedience when in reality the dog doesn't have a clue why he is being "stimulated." The average pet owner is simply not at all equipped to master the science of using this very sophisticated device. There are in fact some experienced professionals who abuse its use, which is further proof that the electronic collar requires dog expertise as well as a calm and rational owner-handler.

The Least You Need To Know

➤ Most problem behaviors are human problems.

➤ Nipping, biting, and aggression are close relatives.

➤ Tackle problem behavior ASAP before it escalates.

➤ You can solve most problem behaviors with patience and common sense.

➤ Seek professional advice if you can't work it out.

➤ Electronic collars can cause more problems than they solve.

Part 4

Healthy Choices

Understanding and training your Golden are just the first part of your new Golden life. Now you have to keep this dog healthy, and that's almost as complicated as training him!

Your dog will live better longer if you, his owner and best friend, know all about health dangers on the dog horizon: diseases and the vaccines that guard against them, the bugs that threaten every dog, hereditary diseases that plague the breed, illnesses and emergencies, and how to recognize and respond to them.

Feeding and grooming your Golden are two more ingredients essential to his long-term health. It's not as simple as just tossing kibble in his food pan. You've heard it here before: smart owners raise smart—and healthy—Goldens.

That's an awful lot to learn, but this is your Golden, and if you hope to enjoy a golden life together, he needs to be in tip-top shape and he needs you to make that happen.

Oops, there's something else. I mention it here so it doesn't get lost in information overload. Every good dog house should own a veterinary medical reference book. You'll use it often to check out health stuff that's too detailed to address in one or two chapters of this book. Only an idiot would be without one!

AH...

Chapter 16

The Two "V"s: Veterinarians and Vaccines

In This Chapter

➤ Finding a good veterinarian

➤ How to visit your veterinarian

➤ Vaccines and diseases

Finding a veterinarian in most U.S. cities is easy. Finding a *good* veterinarian will take a little more time and research. It's worth the extra effort.

This is a major dog decision. You're selecting your Golden's HMO. Your veterinarian must be there for you through sickness and health, hopefully more of the latter than the former. This chapter will help you understand all his ministrations, poking, prodding, and advice.

The Versatile Dog Doctor

Today's veterinarians wear a dozen hats. Many specialize in specific areas of canine health—orthopedics, ophthalmology, oncology, cardiology, nutrition, dermatology, reproduction, internal medicine, acupuncture, holistic medicine—the list goes on. Even the general practitioner vet often has some special area of expertise.

Ask your dog friends (your *smart* dog friends, the ones who take their dog's health seriously) where they go for veterinary care. Ask your breeder or call the secretary of the local kennel club or area Golden Retriever club. If you can, find a veterinary clinic with at least two doctors, more if possible. In an emergency or at the onset of some mysterious ailment, several vet heads are better than one.

Meet the Doc

Select your veterinarian well before your pup's arrival and make his first appointment within his first two or three days of coming home. Your new pup might not be due for a shot, but you'll want a health check anyway, especially if his breeder gave a health guarantee. (Most breeders guarantee a puppy's health for three days to a week.) Bring his health record of all shots and wormings to date, a fresh stool sample in a small clean container, and a pocketful of puppy treats. This veterinary visit is your one exception to "no outings during your puppy's early fear period," so make it a pleasant one.

Bet You Didn't Know

A warm, dry nose does not mean your dog is sick. Cold or wet, warm or dry, both conditions can be normal for a canine.

Important: You and your puppy will wait in the car until the vet can see your pup, and his little paws will not touch the clinic floor. There are too many things lurking there that could infect your puppy. Carry him into the office, place him directly onto the table in the exam room, and pet him lavishly so he's not scared.

If you've chosen wisely, your vet will gush over your puppy to make this visit a positive experience. If your pup is apprehensive, don't coddle or console him; that will only heighten his anxiety. Stay happy and relaxed, and he'll think it's pretty neat to get all this extra hands-on attention.

Bet You Didn't Know

Dogs who eat grass are not sick and do not have worms. Even veterinarians don't know if dogs ingest grass for the moisture content, for a nutritional imbalance, or because of an ancestral instinct. Until research provides an answer, don't worry about it unless it's excessive.

So what's a vet to look at in a bouncing, healthy-looking Golden pup? He will examine all the usual body parts: eyes, ears, throat and glands, genitalia (especially to make sure the testicles have dropped), skin and coat for fleas or flakiness, heart sounds for irregularities, temperature (it will not hurt), and palpate for swollen glands and hernias. All this should be performed with gentle hands so your youngster thinks he's being showered with affection.

Use your dog radar during this first visit. Does the vet's hands-on manner put your pup (and you) at ease? Does he come across as a caring and capable professional? Does he encourage you to ask questions, call him any time? If not, keep looking until you find a vet you're comfortable with.

Doggy Do's

Regardless of my dogs' ages, I always wait in my truck and take them directly into the examining room when it's available. The last dog in the waiting room might have had fleas or parasites, a virus, or a contagious illness. Who needs those problems?

Within a few years, your car will have memorized the route to your vet's office. Your Golden should have, at the very least, an annual check-up to update his shots, annual heartworm test and fecal exam, and a hands-on physical exam. Regular visits also help your vet become familiar with your Golden, which is vital to a solid doctor-canine client relationship. If you ask questions and you keep notes, you can transform these visits from simple routine health care into a Golden learning experience.

Bet You Didn't Know

It is not natural for your dog to have bad breath. Bad breath is a symptom of a health or dental problem. Promote good dental hygiene by offering a dry dog food, hard chew objects, and brush his teeth at least twice a week.

On Pills and Needles

Your puppy's initial health program should include a series of shots and pills for diseases described later in this chapter. Most vaccination schedules consist of a series of injections given at three to four week intervals from six or seven weeks of age through 16 to 20 weeks. He will receive a booster shot of most vaccines at one year of age and annually thereafter throughout his life.

When To Call The Vet

To test for internal bleeding, press your finger against your dog's gums. If the depressed area doesn't return to pink after momentary whiteness, it means that your dog is in shock or has lost a large amount of blood. See your veterinarian at once.

These early shots are critical to your puppy's long-term resistance to canine infection and disease. Puppies are born with an umbrella of antibodies (gifts from their mother) and receive more natural antibodies from the colostrum in her milk. These immunities last through early puppyhood and gradually wear off. Because there is no accurate test to confirm when those immunities are completely gone, puppy shots are scheduled every three to four weeks to provide maximum protection. In recent years, the veterinary profession has offered a vaccine that overrides the dog's natural immunities.

They are given at three-week intervals after six weeks of age. Be sure to ask your vet whether your puppy's shots gave him that protection.

The Immunity Jolt

Vaccine protocol varies from veterinarian to veterinarian. One might give a single injection that combines five, six, seven, or even eight vaccines and covers all the bases. Others prefer separate vaccinations, perhaps giving parvovirus or coronavirus immunizations as separate injections or giving the lepto and Lyme vaccines in the last shot series to minimize the shock to a weak or immature immune system.

That, of course, means a few more visits for each shot. But consider this: just as today's medical world believes we have overdosed on antibiotics and weakened our own immunities, a large segment of the canine medical camp subscribes to that same theory, especially given the increase in cancers and other diseases that were rare in dogs of yore.

I'm of the latter school. I prefer to separate my puppy's shots to allow his little system to recover from each shot. In this chapter, I'll explain each disease and the immunization process.

Alphabet Soup

Your puppy needs a DA₂PP shot plus boosters. Let's break that down into simple understandable English. Each letter represents a component virus of your puppy's shot: D = Canine Distemper, A = Adenovirus type 2 (Hepatitis and cough), P = Parainfluenza, and P = Parvovirus. All are highly contagious, so immunization is a must.

Doggy Do's

To check your dog's pulse, place your fingers flat on the inside of his back thigh where the leg joins the body. The pulsing action should be easy to locate. A normal pulse can range from 70 to 120 beats per minute.

Canine Distemper Virus (CDV)

Viral upper respiratory disease, highly contagious:

➤ Symptoms: Cough, fever, vomiting, diarrhea

➤ Method of exposure: Airborne

Keeping your puppy's vaccines up-to-date is critical to maintaining his good health.

- ➤ Risk: High, usually fatal in puppies

- ➤ Immunizations: Three (3) between 6 and 16 weeks, annual booster

Canine Adenovirus (CA_2)

Viral respiratory, part of kennel cough complex, highly contagious:

- ➤ Symptoms: Harsh, spastic cough

- ➤ Method of exposure: Airborne, saliva

- ➤ Risk: High, possibility of blocked airways and pneumonia, puppies at greatest risk

- ➤ Immunizations: Three (3) between 6 and 16 weeks, annual booster

Infectious Canine Hepatitis (CA₁)

Viral, affects the liver (not related to the hepatitis virus in humans), highly contagious:

➤ Symptoms: Fever, appetite loss, vomiting

➤ Method of exposure: Infected urine, saliva, respiratory discharge, contaminated clothing

➤ Risk: High, puppies at greatest risk

➤ Immunizations: Three (3) between 6 and 16 weeks, annual boosters

Canine Parainfluenza

Viral, respiratory, part of kennel cough complex, highly contagious:

➤ Symptoms: Harsh, spastic cough

➤ Method of exposure: Same as Adenovirus

➤ Risk: High, same potential as Adenovirus, puppies at greatest risk

➤ Immunizations: Three (3) between 6 and 16 weeks, annual boosters

Canine Parvovirus (CPV)

Viral, attacks lining of the intestines:

➤ Symptoms: Bloody or watery diarrhea, fever, vomiting, dehydration, intestinal pain

➤ Method of exposure: Infected feces

➤ Risk: High, usually fatal in puppies

➤ Immunizations: Three (3) between 5 and 16 weeks, annual boosters

171

Leptospirosis

Bacterial, affects kidneys and liver, very contagious:

➤ Symptoms: Fever, appetite loss, bloody stools, listlessness, vomiting, increased thirst

➤ Method of exposure: Urine of infected animals (cattle, sheep, wild animals, rats)

➤ Risk: High in certain areas

➤ Immunizations: One (1), vaccine can produce severe side effects. Immunity short-lived, less than four to six months. Immunize in high-risk areas and after 12 weeks of age.

Canine Coronavirus

Viral, intestinal:

➤ Symptoms: Diarrhea, vomiting, persistent fever

➤ Method of exposure: Infected feces

➤ Risk: Moderate

➤ Immunizations: Two (2) between 6 and 16 weeks, annual booster

Bordatella bronchiseptica

(Canine or kennel cough) viral, respiratory:

➤ Symptoms: Harsh spastic cough, wheezing, fever indicates complications

➤ Method of exposure: Airborne, most common in boarding situations

➤ Risk: High, leads to weakened immune system and secondary bacterial infection

➤ Immunizations: Two (2) intra-nasal or injection between 6 and 16 weeks, annual booster

Lyme (Borreliosis)

Bacterial disease, affects joints:

➤ Symptoms: Lameness, fever, appetite loss, swelling at joints

➤ Risk: High in tick-heavy areas

➤ Method of exposure: Tick bite, at least two species of ticks implicated

➤ Immunization: Controversial at this time, efficacy of vaccine debatable, can produce side effects, use in high-risk areas. Two doses initially, annual booster.

Rabies

Viral, affects central nervous system:

➤ Symptoms: Lack of coordination, seizures, aggression

➤ Risk: *Fatal*

➤ Method of exposure: Saliva, found in some species of wild animals (raccoons, skunk, fox, bat, and others)

➤ Immunization: Once between 12 and 16 weeks, booster every one or three years. Required by all 50 states; can be transmitted to humans.

By now you may be intimidated by the overwhelming responsibility of raising a Golden on this impure, disease-ridden planet. How do you protect him from the dangers lurking on the ground, in the air, the water, in your own back yard? Close your eyes and repeat after me. "I can do this, I can do this." Relax, take a deep breath, and read on.

When To Call The Vet

Coughing can be serious. It's the most common sign of heart disease in canines. If your Golden has been coughing for more than 24 hours, see your veterinarian.

The Least You Need To Know

➤ Find a veterinarian you're comfortable with and trust.

➤ Maximize your visits to the vet.

➤ Understand which shots your Golden does and does not need.

➤ See your veterinarian every year to keep your Golden healthy.

Chapter 17

Inside and Out: The Battle of the Bugs

In This Chapter

➤ Internal parasites

➤ Heartworm disease

➤ External parasites

Bugs, bugs, and more bugs. It's a nasty subject, but you need to know about the more common parasitic critters that can invade or plague your Golden. Like all beasts furry, your dog is a magnet for tiny worms and bugs that could make his life (and yours) slightly miserable to unbearable.

Let's define a parasite. That's an organism that lives in or on a different organism, a host of another character, for its own survival. Sound like an old acquaintance from high school? Some of these little devils often travel, to the bodies of other dogs, and even to people.

The first part of this chapter looks *inside* the dog. I'll talk about seven of these nasty invaders, but the first two parasites account for about 90 percent of all infections.

Roundworms

Roundworms (*toxocara canis*) are the most common parasite found in dogs (and cats, too). They migrate through the lungs, into the bronchial tubes, and then the intestines where they settle for the long term. A heavy infestation will cause a pot-bellied appearance, a dull coat, and poor weight gain, and a heavy infestation can seriously weaken and even kill a very young puppy. Sometimes visible in the stool or vomit, adult roundworms appear as long, spaghetti-like strings. They compete for the dog's dinner, robbing him of valuable nutrition, leading to possible starvation even though the animal is eating large amounts of food.

Most puppies are born with roundworms. Although most adult bitches (healthy ones, that is) don't have active colonies residing in their pregnant bodies, they can pass along the dormant parasites to the whelp still in the womb or through their milk after the birth. The puppies pass the microscopic eggs in their stools, the bitch cleans it up, and the cycle repeats itself. Most breeders worm their pups routinely after three or four weeks of age. Your vet will prescribe a safe wormer depending on the types of parasites found in your puppy's stool.

➤ Symptoms: Dull, dry coat and skin, distended abdomen, loose watery stools, insatiable appetite, dry cough, abdominal discomfort with whimpering or crying.

➤ Treatment: Oral medication in two doses, one for the adult roundworm and a second for the undeveloped larvae.

➤ Prevention: Twice-yearly fecal exams, careful clean-up procedures, and a consistently clean environment. Roundworms can also be controlled with regular use of the heartworm preventative Heartgard Plus, Filarabits Plus, or Interceptor.

Hookworms

Although number two on the parasitic popularity scale, hookworms are the most harmful of all canine intestinal parasites, especially in puppies. Like roundworms, they can be passed through the mother, through fecal contact, and can also enter by burrowing into the animal's exposed skin. They take up residence in the dog's intestines but attach to the intestinal walls to suck blood rather than digesting dog food, resulting in severe anemia and even death in very young pups.

➤ Symptoms: Bloody diarrhea, a dull, dry coat, weight loss, weakness, distended abdomen, and insatiable appetite. In otherwise healthy adult dogs, no symptoms might appear.

➤ Treatment: Oral medication in two doses.

➤ Prevention: Twice yearly fecal exams and a strict sanitary environment. Hookworms can be controlled with regular use of the heartworm preventative Heartgard Plus, Filarabits Plus, or Interceptor.

Tapeworms

Tapeworms come from fleas. Dogs can get one of six types of tapeworms by eating an infected flea or an intermediate host: a rodent, bird, or critter (or part of one) that carries the flea. (Goldens are notorious for gobbling up dead birds and bunny parts.) Tapeworms look like wiggly grains of rice. Many dog owners discover their dog is infected when they see the worm segments in the dog's stool, or in a worse-case scenario, crawling in his anal area. Tapeworm segments can also contaminate rugs and furniture and the dog's bedding.

➤ Symptoms: Increased appetite and weight loss, alternating diarrhea and constipation, and chewing at the rectal area. Healthy adult dogs might show no signs other than mild diarrhea. In my own experience with tapeworm (which is considerable because I live in the country, and my Goldens are forever foraging for some dead or rotting animal part), my dogs have never developed diarrhea, but I'm sure that that is because I find them *early*; not to brag, but I'm *always* looking at their stools!

➤ Treatment: Oral medication.

➤ Prevention: Rigid flea control that includes frequent inspection of fresh stools ("Ooohh, what a good potty break today!"), and a sanitary dog and people environment. Don't allow your Golden to eat potential host creatures. Good luck with that one!

Whipworms

Dogs acquire whipworms by ingesting the eggs through either direct fecal contact or microscopic fecal matter on their coat or feet. Whipworms are tough to diagnose and might require more than one fecal exam. They are also very resistant to many disinfectants used to destroy the larvae. (One old-time breeder advises a generous dose of plain old table salt sprinkled generously in the kennel and potty areas. It works, although it is obviously not practical throughout the yard!)

➤ Symptoms: Watery, slimy, or bloody diarrhea that can be intermittent, increased appetite, weight loss, a dull, dry coat, abdominal pain.

➤ Treatment: Oral medication.

➤ Prevention: Keep the dog's living area clean and dry with good exposure to sunlight. The heartworm preventative Interceptor or Filarabits Plus is also effective at preventing whipworms.

Heartworm

This is one disease that's far worse than the bite that causes it. Heartworm occurs when an infective mosquito bites your dog and deposits the heartworm larvae into the animal's bloodstream. The larvae migrate to the body tissues where they spend three or four months maturing into small adult worms. From there they make their way into a vein, move to the heart, and set up housekeeping in the right side of the heart as sexually mature worms. Of course, they mate inside the heart, and the female can produce up to 5,000 microfilariae in a single day. That colony will sit and wait for the next mosquito bite so they can hop a ride and continue the same life cycle in another dog.

The adult heartworms will reach lengths of 4 to 12 inches in the heart and arteries of the lungs. The result is obvious: decreased circulation, heart failure, and, ultimately, your own heartbreak.

➤ Symptoms of heartworm disease might not appear for up to a year or longer after infection first occurs. The most constant sign is a soft, deep cough that gets worse with exercise. The dog will become listless and tire easily, lose weight, his coat will become dry and dull, and he might cough up bloody sputum. Treatment is expensive and risky, but without it, the dog will die.

➤ Heartworm medication will prevent the disease.

➤ Daily or monthly pills are available through your veterinarian, but the dog must first be tested for the disease before taking the preventive. Why? The medication will kill any microfilaria present, and if there are large numbers, they will die and clog his lungs and blood vessels. People who live in warm climates where mosquitoes thrive all year should keep their dogs on year-round medication.

Your puppy was born free of heartworm. He needs to start a daily or monthly puppy-size preventive with your first visit to your vet.

Giardia

This little monster is a one-celled parasite passed through fecal ingestion (eating infected stools) or through drinking infected water in public areas. It attaches to the dog's intestinal wall and can be especially disastrous in very young pups. Giardia is capable of passing from cattle to dogs, dogs to humans, and so on down the contagion chain.

➤ Symptoms: Severe watery or persistent diarrhea and dehydration.

➤ Treatment includes long-term medication, and reinfection is not uncommon. The parasite is hard to diagnose because it shrinks after shedding in the stool and might not be present or detectable in every stool sample.

➤ Prevention: The most effective prevention is through strict sanitation in the dog's living area and by avoiding contact with possible contamination in lakes and ponds frequented by wildlife.

Coccidia

These one-celled organisms pack a wallop that belies their size. My introduction to coccidia was brutal when three pups in my four-week-old litter of Goldens suddenly became listless and presented watery yellow diarrhea. After three high-speed runs to my veterinarian, several days of subcutaneous (under the skin) hydration, and round-the-clock neo-natal care, we all prevailed triumphant, although I was by then considerably weaker than the pups!

Coccidia is spread through the feces or through contaminated food or water, or can be passed from a nursing dam to her whelp. It develops quickly in the dog or pup's intestines. Diagnosis requires fresh stools and special testing procedures designed to reveal this type of parasite.

➤ Symptoms: Loose, watery stools, listlessness, vomiting, weight loss.

➤ Treatment: Oral medication containing sulfadimethoxine in pill or liquid form. It must be quick and aggressive, but is usually successful.

➤ Prevention: More of the same: conscientious hygiene in a dry, clean living environment with good exposure to sunlight.

Be a Hygiene Fanatic

You can't be too careful. Keep your dog and dog areas scrupulously clean. Have your veterinarian do twice-yearly fecal exams and call him immediately if your dog shows any of the warning signs: diarrhea, fatigue, vomiting, weight loss, or bloating. Always consult your vet before using any anti-parasite product on your dog or his environment.

As if it's not bad enough that you and your poor dog might have to deal with creepy crawlers on his inside, there's more. External parasites include fleas, ticks, and other mighty mites.

Fleas

Even the cave dog probably had a run-in with some flea bag now and then. Holding steady as the first and foremost canine adversary, the flea, along with the cockroach, has outmaneuvered all attempts at extermination. Check out this scary statistic. Under the right conditions (warm and humid), one adult flea can produce 25,000 fleas in 30 days.

It's almost guaranteed that you and your dog will encounter fleas at least once during your dog's lifetime. If you hope to wage a winning battle, you first must understand the enemy.

Adult fleas that have had their first blood meal must dine every 24 hours in order to survive. For that reason and their own convenience, most adult fleas will remain on their food source, which is your dog or other warm-blooded animal.

The majority of the flea population—the eggs (which will hatch into first-stage larvae within 21 days), the first stage larvae (which will mature into second-stage pupae from 9 to 200 days), and second-stage pupae (which can become adults in just a few days or take as long as nine months, depending on their food source)—will live in the environment rather than on the dog. Most eggs are laid on the dog, and then fall off into your carpet, bedding, furniture, or grass, where they move along in their life cycle. (Makes you start to itch all over, doesn't it?)

With such huge numbers and so many life stages, this is a tough war with several strategies. Fortunately, flea prevention and eradication has become easier, thanks to modern dog-science. Today, in addition to traditional flea management, several revolutionary new flea weapons put effective flea control in every dog house.

Fipronil—Frontline

Fipronil is a safe adulticide (a product that disables the flea's nervous system) marketed under the name of Frontline. It comes in a spray or a spot-on treatment that is applied to the dog's skin between the shoulder blades, providing 100 percent control within 24 hours. The dog, however, must be kept dry for about 48 hours after application. The best part for water dogs like Goldens is that Fipronil is water–friendly, and your dog can swim without reducing its effectiveness. Fipronil does not enter the dog's bloodstream; it spreads across the body through the hair follicles and oil glands in the skin, killing fleas within four hours of contact and ticks within 12 hours.

181

(Blessedly, the flea does not have to bite the dog.) One application will control fleas for up to 90 days on dogs and will control ticks for up to 30 days. It's safe for puppies and provides better protection than the combined use of collar, sprays, and premise treatments.

Imidacloporid—Advantage

Advantage is a safe spot-on treatment applied between the shoulder blades that quickly spreads, as does Frontline, across the surface of the dog's skin. Also an adulticide, it kills 98 to 100 percent of adult fleas within 24 hours. It is not absorbed into the dog's bloodstream and remains effective for 30 days.

Lufenuron—Program

Commonly known as "the monthly flea pill," Lufenuron is an insect growth regulator (IGR) marketed under the name of Program. It prevents the flea eggs from hatching, thus breaking the flea life cycle. Although Program is essentially non-toxic, it does not prevent flea bites, which are a problem for the flea-allergic dog.

Traditional Flea Remedies

Traditional remedies now take a back seat to the popular and less toxic products such as those mentioned earlier. Nevertheless, they're still out there on the market, and you should know their names and the dangers they pose to your dog.

If fleas could read, they'd probably be proud of all the products devoted to their extermination. Here's a flea dictionary of terms and over-the-counter and prescription remedies that supplement the IGRs and adulticides.

➤ *Amitraz.* A toxic chemical used in tick collars. It kills ticks, not fleas, and can be used in combination with other flea and tick products. (Many others cannot.)

➤ *Organophosphates and carbamates.* Toxic chemicals still used in many flea-killing products. They are absorbed into the animal's system and can be fatal, especially if mixed with certain other flea products. Use with extreme caution. If you don't know what the ingredient is, don't guess; ask your veterinarian.

➤ *Pyrethins.* A natural plant extract from the chrysanthemum family found in Africa. Easily metabolized when taken orally, so it offers low toxicity to pets.

➤ *Permethrins.* A synthetic pyrethin with longer residual action, commonly used with quick-killing natural pyrethins to control fleas and ticks. Permethrins and pyrethins are faster-acting adult flea killers with low to moderate residual effects (retained in the dog's system).

➤ *Flea collars.* Insecticides are time-released from the collars and will not control a serious flea infestation. May cause allergic reactions due to long-term exposure to low levels of insecticides. Always remove prior to bathing and *never* combine with dips or sprays.

➤ *Sprays and powders.* Easily applied, but must be used often. Will not penetrate oily or heavy coats. Ineffective in serious infestations.

➤ *Shampoos.* Will kill fleas if properly used, but little residual effect.

➤ *Dips.* More insecticides. Dips are more effective and offer more residual effect, but they are also quite toxic. Best (safest) handled by your veterinarian.

➤ *Combs.* Flea combs have 32 tiny teeth per inch. Useful for short-term removal, but difficult to use on heavy or long-coated dogs.

➤ *Systemics.* May be oral or topical. May be insecticide or growth regulators, both of which enter the dog's system to kill fleas or prevent maturation of eggs.

➤ *Premise sprays.* Applied to the house or yard to kill adult fleas or inhibit larvae growth.

➤ *Foggers.* More effective indoors than outside. Will not kill adult or pre-adult fleas or flea eggs. Must remove animals and protect food and utensils. Penetration limited by furniture.

Confused? Ask your veterinarian!

If at all possible, avoid using pesticide sprays and dips that contain organophosphates and carbamates because they are highly toxic.

Products containing natural pyrethins are less toxic (relatively speaking) and therefore a better choice.

Doggy Don'ts

Never combine flea preventives (flea dip with a flea collar, topical flea spray with oral medication, and so on) without first checking with your vet. Example: never place a flea collar on a dog that has been recently bathed, dipped, or sprayed with a pesticide. Some of those chemical combinations can be fatal!

Get the jump on fleas and start prevention before they find your dog. Use a three-pronged attack that covers your dog, your house, and your yard.

Dog

Consult your veterinarian and use whatever flea preventative he or she recommends. Groom your dog with a flea comb (dipped in soapy water to snag and drown the fleas) after every trip outdoors and use it at least weekly to check for fleas and flea dirt. If you find suspicious dark specks on his underside between his hind legs or on his back at the base of his tail, rub them with a moist tissue. Flea dirt will turn a reddish brown color.

House

Routinely vacuum and clean all floors, furniture, and beds, especially areas where your Golden sleeps, plays, or rests.

Doggy Do's

Drop a two-inch section of a flea collar in the vacuum bag to kill any fleas or larvae you might pick up.

This simple household chore (simple depending on who's doing the chore!) is more effective than pesticides in controlling fleas. Read the label *and ask your vet* before using carpet sprays or household foggers. Some of those products can cause toxicity problems that are worse than fleas.

After walking in a field and other wildlife areas, always do a thorough check for ticks and fleas.

The Yard

This is harder. Remove any debris and spray with an IGR. If you have a serious flea problem and the area's too big to handle on your own, use a lawn service. If you can't afford one, ask your vet for more affordable remedies.

Ticks

Modern science has yet to discover why ticks were created in the first place. These ugly bloodsuckers are everywhere, just waiting for some warm-blooded creature to hop on to. Ticks are major carriers of disease and must be removed as soon as possible to prevent infection. If you spend time outdoors or in the woods, check your dog—and yourself—twice daily. Ticks love warm, moist places, so confine your walks and play to open, sunny areas. Use a spot-on tick preventive, a tick collar, or a spray. Check with your vet before using two tick products at the same time.

Safe tick removal is also important. You want to avoid crushing the tick so its bloody contents don't spurt out and contaminate you or your dog. Use a tweezers or tissue to gently pull the tick straight out (not up) from the bite site. Spray it first with a bit of flea spray or alcohol to make it loosen its mouth parts that are attached to the skin. Drop the body in a jar of alcohol or bleach or flush it down the toilet.

185

Bet You Didn't Know

A clever little gadget called Pro-tick remedy is the easiest and safest means of tick removal. It always (well, almost always) gets the head out, too. You can order one from Safety Consulting Services (SCS) Ltd., P.O. Box 573, Stony Point, NY 10980. 800-PIX-TICK (749-8425).

Tick-Borne Diseases

These diseases are nonpartisan and affect people as well as dogs.

Lyme Disease (Borrelia Burfdorferi)

Named for the Connecticut city of Lyme where it was first discovered in 1977, Lyme disease is found today in every state. The current vaccine for this disease is still controversial, so the best protection against infection is still prevention.

Spread through at least two species of the tiny deer tick, Lyme attacks dogs as aggressively as it attacks humans, invading the joints and causing painful swelling, lameness, and lethargy. Prolonged exposure can cause permanent damage to the heart and kidneys, so prompt treatment is important. False positives are common in the testing process, and your veterinarian might have to run two or three titer tests to confirm a diagnosis. Several weeks of the antibiotic tetracycline is the most common treatment.

Lyme arthritis is the most treatable form of the disease, but many affected dogs will have recurring symptoms even after treatment. Cardiac and neurological disorders will respond to antibiotics, but kidney Lyme disease is almost always fatal.

For more information about Lyme disease, contact the Lyme Disease Foundation Inc. at 800-886-LYME, a 24-hour hotline.

Canine Ehrlichiosis

Similar to the tick-borne Lyme disease, ehrlichiosis is transmitted through the bite of the Brown Dog Tick, with at least one other tick species under suspicion as a carrier. The disease attacks the blood platelets and might produce Lyme-type symptoms of mild fever, appetite loss, swollen lymph nodes, nose bleeds, and abnormal discharge from the eyes and/or nose. The symptoms might come and go, making an accurate diagnosis difficult. Current treatment involves aggressive use of antibiotics, and affected dogs are more prone to reinfection. Erlichia is more common in tick-prone areas, so tick control is still the best preventive measure.

Bet You Didn't Know

In 1994 ehrlichiosis was also discovered in humans. It can be fatal in both dogs and people, with advanced stages causing kidney failure and respiratory problems, which makes early diagnosis critical.

Rocky Mountain Spotted Fever

The name of this disease implies its origin and whereabouts. Symptoms of RMSF include fever, bloody urine, and loose or bloody stools, breathing difficulty, and unexplained nose bleeds that usually occur within two weeks of contracting the illness. See your veterinarian for titer tests to confirm infection.

Mites

Moving again along the parasitic chain, mites are less visible than ticks but just as pesky. Mites are microscopic eight-legged parasites that love to feast on the various body parts of the dog.

Ear Mites

Adult ear mites settle into the lining of the ear canal, causing irritation and extreme itching. Your dog will scratch and dig and try to shove his paw into his ear. He will shake his head a lot and maybe even walk a little crooked. Mites usually produce a smelly, brownish wax (in the ear—where else?) which your vet will examine under the microscope to find the mites.

A regimen of six to eight weeks of ear drops will squelch the infestation. Mites are transmitted by direct contact and are highly contagious, so they are often shared with other canine family members. If one of your Goldens has ear mites, have everyone in your dog family checked by your vet and give each one a thorough mite-specific shampoo to whack any stray pests that might be wandering around on the dogs.

Mange Mites

There are three cousins in this family, each one rendering its own brand of havoc on your dog.

Sarcoptic Mange

Sarcoptes (also known as scabies) can be devastating. This crab-shaped mite burrows under the dog's skin to lay its eggs, causing continuous intense itching. The infected animal will be miserable and scratch, dig, and literally chew himself raw until much of his body is scabby and hairless. The damage is often compounded by secondary bacterial infections resulting from the open sores.

Scabies mites are microscopic and might require several deep skin scrapings to confirm their presence. Your vet might prescribe a series of dips or injections. Scabies is highly contagious to humans as well as other dogs, so if you develop an itchy rash around your midsection, call your physician as well as your vet.

Demodectic Mange

Considered by some to be the scourge of the mange family, demodex is sometimes called "red mange" or "puppy mange." Passed to puppies during the nursing process, demodex usually exist harmlessly in the animal's hair follicles and oil glands.

Then all of a sudden—Boom! Somehow one or more pups become stressed for who knows why, and the mites multiply in the coat, causing bare patches around the eyes, face, neck, and front legs. If itching occurs, scratching can lead to secondary bacterial infections of the skin, further stressing the young victim's immature immune system.

Early diagnosis and treatment are important to keep the demodex under control and localized. That includes superb health care and a stress-free environment to minimize the impact on the pup's immune system.

Despite an owner's best efforts, about 10 percent of localized demodex cases progress into generalized demodex due to decreased immuno-competence. A normal immune system should resolve spontaneously. The hair loss will spread across the puppy's body, causing inflamed and itchy bald patches, secondary infections, and a serious condition called deep pyoderma. Generalized demodex is extremely difficult to control, requiring special bathing, dips, and antibiotics, all while the animal is in great pain due to skin damage from the demodex. Euthanasia is not ruled out as a last resort. Thank goodness this condition is not contagious.

Because there is a strong hereditary predisposition for generalized demodex, all dogs with the disease should be sterilized. In fact, some experts recommend that parents and siblings of affected dogs also be removed from breeding programs to protect future generations from the agony of the disease.

Chyletiella Mites

These dandruff mites are often called "walking dandruff" because they travel and nibble across the surface of the skin, causing mild itching and flaking on the head and along the back, and your dog will bite and scratch those areas. Your vet can control the condition with prescription dips and follow-up shampoos or sprays to target any leftover mites that escape the treatment.

The Least You Need to Know

➤ Check your Golden's stool for parasites—all the time!

➤ Your Golden will need an annual heartworm test and preventive medication.

➤ Guard against fleas and be extra careful of flea killers and preventives.

➤ Take every tick precaution possible.

➤ Be alert for tiny mites that could infect your dog.

Chapter 18

In Sickness and in Health

In This Chapter

➤ Allergy wars: itch, scratch, wheeze, and sneeze

➤ Everyday ailments

➤ Emergency situations and first aid

➤ A healthy, golden grin

Sorry to bring you the bad news, but Golden Retrievers share health problems common in most dogs. Too bad. But since we can't fight Mother Nature, we have to be smart enough to fight the problems when they arise. And a dedicated Golden owner is automatically a smart dog owner!

Allergies

Our lovely Golden Retrievers are one of several breeds that are highly predisposed to allergies. Some allergies are seasonal, some appear at various life stages, and some skin diseases become lifelong problems requiring frequent or continuous treatment by a veterinarian.

Dogs with allergies don't *usually* sneeze or get runny noses as people do. (A few do, however.) Instead, they itch and scratch, chew, lick and rub their feet, ears, belly, and any part of their body they can reach. Left untreated, the irritated skin becomes traumatized and damaged and subsequently infected. The most common types of allergens are flea saliva, inhaled substances (pollen, mold, dust) and food ingredients.

Flea Allergies

The most common and most debilitating allergy is flea allergy dermatitis, which is a hypersensitivity to the protein in flea saliva. It's most commonly diagnosed after age two, is most severe from mid-summer through fall, and always requires veterinary care. In warmer climates, it can be a year-round plague.

In flea-allergic dogs, it takes only one tiny flea bite to set a major allergy machine in motion. Flea allergic dogs will scratch and bite themselves raw, with most of the intense itching and biting occurring near the base of the tail. Your veterinarian will prescribe anti-inflammatory medication, an oral or spot-on flea preventive medication, and also recommend stringent flea control that includes the environment (house and yard) as well as the dog. Routine grooming, brushing, and thorough body inspections are also vital for flea allergy preventive maintenance.

Medical Management

Topical remedies can provide short-term relief, but they don't address the problem. Shampoos, rinses, anti-itch sprays, and soaks between baths can help make an itchy dog more comfortable.

Cortisone and other steroids will make your dog feel better, but they are a quick fix that will not make allergies go away. They also have other potentially damaging side effects, so they should never be used long term. Antihistamines can offer relief from certain inhalant allergies. Additives containing omega 3 and omega 6 fatty acids often help because they block the inflammation that causes the itching.

Desensitization is a slow, expensive process, and although a large percentage of dogs improve, there's no guarantee it will work.

Summertime Blues

If you own a Golden, you probably know of, or will experience, hot spots. These are painful, moist, infected areas on the skin that may develop from repeated scratching or appear out of the blue for no reason at all and enlarge rapidly. One day you brush your Golden, and underneath the long hair on some body part you find an oozing, hairless sore. A hot spot can be horrific. Tackle it immediately before it spreads.

Hot Spot Treatment

Clip the hair to eliminate the damp undersurface and cleanse (carefully—it will probably hurt) with an antiseptic wash and dilute hydrogen peroxide. Apply one of several topical ointments several times a day. Experienced Golden owners have used the following successfully: Sulfadene (from your pharmacy), Wonder Dust (a horse powder found in most feed and grain stores and tack shops), and apple cider vinegar (my personal favorite). All are drying agents with healing properties. I know one veterinarian/Golden breeder who swears by Sea Breeze astringent.

The "No Lick" Command

You must somehow prevent your dog from licking or gnawing at the hot spot wound. Spray a little Bitter Apple around the wound (never on it!) or use an Elizabethan collar if necessary. If you don't see improvement in a few days, see your vet, or you'll soon have a secondary infection to deal with.

Lick Spots

Officially called acral lick dermatitis (ALD), lick sores are born through excessive licking of one spot, usually

> **Doggy Do's**
>
> Always check your Golden for hot spots and other coat irregularities after a stay at a boarding kennel or if he's been swimming a lot. Some golden coats take forever to dry, and a constant damp coat provides a perfect host site for a hot spot.

the front of one or both legs or feet. ALD sometimes starts with a minor injury, a bee sting, splinter, or irritation the dog licks and chews, and then continues licking long after the wound has healed. The resulting aggravation might be due to boredom, stress, or some environmental change known only to the dog.

When To Call The Vet

Internal bleeding can be insidious. You might not discover it until the situation is critical. External symptoms include blood in the vomit or the urine, pale pink or white-ish gums, and listlessness.

If you can prevent the licking with anti-chewing sprays, or in desperation with an Elizabethan collar, the spot should heal on its own. A few dogs, however, persist and go back to licking the healed area or start working on a new one. Get creative, keep your Golden busy, and ask your vet for more advice.

Bloat Notes

We're all familiar with the human version of bloat. Too much Thanksgiving dinner, too many mashed potatoes. Not quite so with dogs.

Bloat—or GVD (gastric dilation volvulus)—is a build-up of gas that can't escape from the dog's stomach. As the gas accumulates, the stomach swells and will quickly twist, blocking food passage in or out of the stomach and blood flow to other internal organs. The dog is in great pain and on the brink of shock and death within the hour.

Large breeds such as Great Danes, Irish Setters, and retrievers are most affected, especially dogs who eat large meals, eat once a day, or gulp their food. Symptoms of bloat are sudden discomfort paired with labored breathing, restlessness, roaching the back, drooling and unproductive vomiting, and abdominal swelling. Tapping the dog's sides will produce a hollow sound. Get veterinary attention ASAP, or your dog will die!

Preventive measures make good common dog sense. Divide your dog's food into two smaller meals a day and feed dry kibble with water added. Avoid strenuous exercise for one hour before and two hours after a meal (same as swimmers' rules).

For Girls Only: Pyometra

Pyometra is generally an "old lady" disease and shows up in unspayed bitches over five years of age. The uterus becomes filled with pus, usually after her estrus cycle. Pyometra can be fatal if not caught in time, and spay surgery is usually the only medical solution. Obviously, spayed bitches are never at risk—another good reason to have your Golden girl spayed.

Doggy Do's

Research at Purdue University shows that underweight, fearful, and nervous dogs are at higher risk for GVD. (Fear, nervousness, and excitement all increase air swallowing in humans.) A happy dog is less likely to get GVD. Message: Keep your Golden happy, and you'll keep him healthy, too!

Diarrhea

There's diarrhea, and then there's *diarrhea*! Loose stools can be due to a dozen things from a sudden change in diet or drinking water, emotional upset or excitement, scavenging in the garbage, parasites or other serious problem, or disease. Examine the stool for color, consistency, odor, and frequency, and keep a record for your vet. A bout that persists for more than 24 hours, a bloody diarrhea, and diarrhea accompanied by vomiting, fever, or other signs of toxicity should send your dog directly to his doctor.

You can treat ordinary diarrhea at home. Withhold all food for 24 hours. Offer small amounts of water or ice cubes for your dog's thirst. Give him Kaopectate (same weight dose as humans) or Immodium AD, one capsule per 50 pounds of dog. Resume feeding with small amounts of a no-fat diet: one part boiled hamburger to two parts cooked rice, cottage cheese, or cooked pasta. Follow for two or three days before returning your dog to his regular diet.

Vomiting

Follow the same premise as for diarrhea. You need to watch *how* your Golden vomits and notice *what* he vomits. Most vomiting is due to overeating or eating grass or some other tasty indigestible stuff.

Doggy Do's

Secure your outdoor garbage cans with tight lids and keep your compost pile well out of reach. Rotting garbage smells like haute cuisine to most dogs. Your dog can die from eating bacteria-ridden garbage.

When should you worry? If the vomiting is repeated, sporadic with no relationship to meals, bloody, forceful, and projectile (any of these), always seek veterinary help. If the vomit contains feces or foreign matter or is accompanied by drooling, whining, or trembling, get to the veterinarian ASAP.

Should You Induce Vomiting?

Your Golden has just swallowed a package of mouse bait. (I know this is fantasy because you'd never make that mistake, so this is strictly hypothetical.) Should you make him throw up the bad stuff, or should you rush him to the vet for a swallowing emergency? If unsure, call the National Animal Poison Control Center: 1 (800) 548-2428 or 1 (888) 4ANIHELP. This organization takes calls 24 hours a day.

However, you should know *not* to induce vomiting if your dog:

➤ Swallows an acid, a solvent, or other toxic cleaner

➤ Swallows a petroleum product (gasoline, turpentine, and so on)

➤ Swallows a sharp object (which could perforate his esophagus or stomach on the way back up)

➤ Is comatose, or more than two hours has passed since he ate the poison

You can induce vomiting by giving 3 percent hydrogen peroxide every 10 minutes (one teaspoon for every 20 pounds of dog; use a turkey baster poked to the rear of his throat). You can also give syrup of ipecac at one teaspoon per 10 pounds of dog.

Urinary Incontinence

This is inappropriate passing of urine, usually unintentional, although sometimes not. Owners will complain that their dog leaks urine when relaxed. It typically occurs in older, spayed females, although neutered males can be affected, too. Old age = weak urethral sphincter muscle. Most cases respond well to drug therapy, but if the underlying cause is renal failure, diabetes, or other abnormality, your vet will have to perform tests to make an accurate diagnosis.

Don't confuse incontinence with some male dog's tendency to lift his leg and "sprinkle" every bush even after he's relieved himself. This "marking" system is behavioral and not at all related to his bladder.

Signs of Good and Poor Health

Your Golden should be the picture of perfect health, but what does that look like? From nose to toes, here are your dog's body signs.

Temperature

A dog's normal body temperature is 100.5° to 101.5°F. Take your dog's temperature with a rectal thermometer or "instant" digital thermometer that "dings" when done. Dip the bulb into petroleum jelly, lift the tail, and gently insert the bulb into the anus. Be meticulous about your hygiene!

Heart

At rest, canines register 90 to 100 beats per minute, with puppies and senior dogs a little faster. You can feel your dog's heartbeat on the inner side of the hind leg and just behind the flex of the front leg.

Nose

Your Golden's nose should be black and smooth, never crusted or cracked. Nose note: A dry, warm, wet, or cold nose is not a dog's health barometer.

Ears

The inner flap and ear canal should be pink and free of wax and debris. A smelly or waxy substance or discharge indicates ear mites or an infection. See Chapter 19 for ear cleaning instructions.

Teeth

Your Golden's teeth should be white and free of plaque. Offer hard, sterile bones and hard rubber bones to chew his way to dental health.

When To Call The Vet

Always call your vet if:
- You find a lump any-where on your Golden's skin
- Your Golden seems unusually short of breath
- Your Golden becomes uncharacteristically fearful or aggressive

Gums

Gums should be firm and pink with the edges closely applied to the teeth. Some pigmentation or dark spots are normal. A black spot on the tongue is also common. Very pale gums reflect a lowered body temperature and could mean hypothermia or other serious illness or disease. Bright red gums are a sign of elevated body temperature and the onset of heat stroke, which is life threatening and requires imme-diate emergency measures.

Skin

Your dog's skin should be supple without scaling or flaking; his coat should be thick and shiny, although many variations exist in length, texture, and density.

First Aid Kit	
First aid instruction book	Syrup of ipecac to induce vomiting
Gauze (2- and 3-inch pads)	
Adhesive tape	Kaopectate to control diarrhea (Immodium AD also works for dogs)
Vet wrap (a stick-to-itself gauze bandage wrap)	
Cotton swabs	Eye wash
Hydrogen peroxide and alcohol	Rectal thermometer
	Tweezers
Panalog or other antibiotic ointment	Eye dropper

Syringe without the needle to give oral medications

Ascriptin 325 mg (Tylenol is not good for dogs)

Tourniquet (a wide rubber band and a pencil will do)

Muzzle (use a leash, tie, or pantyhose)

Benadryl or Benadryl elixir for allergic reactions (always check first with your veterinarian for the correct dose; generally one tablet for every 25 pounds)

Towels, one per animal in a vehicle (it can be wet with water or alcohol to cool an overheated dog)

Blanket (one per vehicle to use as a stretcher or for treating shock)

Large water container for traveling (an absolute necessity in summer)

Your veterinarian's office and emergency telephone number

Emergency Situations

Your first aid kit is just a start. You have to be prepared. This is like taking your emergency SATs.

Doggy Do's

Every Golden owner should have a well-planned emergency kit for the home (it can serve double duty for your family) plus a backup kit for the car if your Golden frequently tags along for the ride. Check with your veterinarian for specific items, but those in the chart should give you a good start.

Heatstroke

Dogs overheat more easily than we humans do because they aren't blessed with our sweat glands. They cool off through their footpads and by panting, neither of which is very efficient. All breeds are vulnerable to heatstroke, but puppies, older dogs, and overweight dogs are most susceptible. To help prevent heatstroke, do not leave your dog tied up all day where he will be exposed to the sun. (Dogs left in outdoor kennels or yards need all-day shade and a constant supply of cool water.) Do not allow your dog to overexert himself on a hot day. (The elevated temperature can cause coma, brain damage, and an extremely painful death.) And finally, never, *ever* leave your Golden in a closed car during warm weather. In spring through early fall, the inside of a car, even with windows cracked several inches on a breezy 75-degree day, can heat to over 120 degrees in minutes. A confined animal will suffer heatstroke and die an excruciating death. That extra five minutes in Wal-Mart could be fatal. Leave your Golden at home!

Symptoms of Heatstroke

The following are symptoms of heatstroke:

➤ Excessive panting

➤ Drooling

➤ Rapid pulse

➤ Dark red gums and tongue

➤ A frantic, glazed expression

➤ Possibly vomiting

When To Call The Vet

• Your Golden has an abrupt change in appetite, up or down.

• Your Golden starts losing weight for no apparent reason.

• Your Golden drinks more water and urinates more frequently.

Treat the symptoms immediately and then rush your dog to the vet to continue emergency care. Cool him down by immersing him in a pond or a tub of cool water (not cold) or hosing him down with a garden hose. Put ice around his neck and groin and offer ice cubes to lick but no ice water to drink. A body temperature over 106°F requires a cold water enema to reduce the temperature immediately. Immediate follow-up vet care is urgent, because the body temperature can rise again very quickly during the next 48 hours.

The best cure is prevention: keep your canine cool.

Wingers and Stingers

Most stings are painful, but they are rarely dangerous unless your Golden suffers an allergic reaction when he's stung. If he's allergic, his face, and possibly his legs, will swell. He might get the chills and a fever, have difficulty breathing, and go into shock. Be alert for signs of discomfort or distress and take him to the vet immediately. Over the counter antihistamines can buffer an allergic response, but ask your veterinarian what to use and how much.

Burns

Electrical shock and burns are most common in puppies that chew, chew, chew on appliance or extension cords, but don't rule out a curious adult Golden. If the burn is severe, the dog will incur tissue damage and retain fluid in his lungs. If he's unconscious and not breathing, give artificial respiration and get immediate veterinary attention.

Thermal burns are caused by contact with open flames, boiling water, stoves, and any heated object or surface. First apply ice packs or ice water for 20 to 30 minutes. Follow with a soothing antibiotic ointment twice daily and make sure the dog doesn't lick it off.

For a caustic acid or chemical burn, flush immediately and liberally with cool water. Apply an antibiotic preparation and ice to reduce swelling. Prevent the dog from licking the injured area. Always check with your vet after any type of burn.

Animal Bites

Bites are typically puncture wounds that are heavily contaminated and likely to become infected. Most vets advise against suturing and prefer to cleanse the area and treat with antibiotics.

Bleeding

Bleeding can be arterial (the spurting of bright red blood) or venous (oozing of dark red blood) or sometimes both. Both require immediate veterinary attention. Your pet is in danger from shock, coma, and death. Picture your dog's bleeding wound on a child to help determine your emergency situation.

Superficial cuts and scratches should be kept clean and dry to prevent infection. Fresh lacerations over ½ inch deep or long should be sutured to prevent infection and scarring and to speed healing.

Doggy Don'ts

When it comes to bleeding, there are two *don'ts* to remember. Do not pour peroxide on a fresh wound. That will make the bleeding harder to control. Do not wipe a wound that has stopped bleeding because that could dislodge the blood clot that has formed.

Shock

Shock is the lack of adequate blood flow to support the body's needs. It's caused by a sudden loss of blood, heatstroke, poisoning, dehydration from prolonged vomiting or diarrhea, or severe trauma such as being hit by a car. If not treated quickly, the animal will die.

Symptoms of shock are a drop in body temperature, shivering, listlessness and mental depression, and a weak, faint pulse. Keep the dog calm and comfortable, cover him lightly with a coat or blanket, and get to the nearest veterinarian immediately.

Dehydration

This is an excessive loss of body fluids caused by fever, inadequate water intake, or prolonged vomiting and/or diarrhea. The most common sign of dehydration is a lack of skin elasticity. Pinch up the skin along the back of the dog's neck. If it remains up in a tent, that's evidence of dehydration.

You can treat a mild case of dehydration with electrolyte fluids given by mouth. If the dog won't drink copious amounts of water or electrolyte fluids, your veterinarian will give fluids by syringe.

Frostbite and Hypothermia

Just because your Golden has a long fur coat and loves the snow doesn't mean that he's not at risk for either of these serious conditions. Dogs of all breeds can get frostbite just as people do. Dogs exposed to wet or very cold conditions are prime candidates for frozen body parts.

A severe trauma, such as being hit by a car, can cause a dog to go into shock. Keep the dog calm and comfortable and get him to the veterinarian's office immediately.

What to look for? Frostbitten areas will be very cold and pale and might have a bluish cast, followed soon by redness and swelling. Ears, tails, and genitals are the most susceptible areas.

Gently warm the affected areas without rubbing (you can do more damage), use a heating pad on the low setting or warm—not hot—compresses, and see your veterinarian as soon as possible.

Hypothermia is even more dangerous. Prolonged exposure to the cold, especially if the dog is wet, will cause a dangerous drop in body temperature. Your dog will shiver and might appear disoriented or lethargic, even collapse. His rectal temperature will fall below 97 degrees.

If the dog is wet, give him a quick warm bath and rub vigorously with towels to dry his fur. Slowly rewarm him using a hair dryer on the lowest setting. Offer him a warm drink and warm him under blankets, with your own body heat if possible. You can also apply warm water packs or heating pads to the armpits, chest, and abdomen until his body temperature rises to 100°F. Then take him to the veterinarian as soon as possible.

203

Doggy Don'ts

Indoor living does not prepare a dog or his coat for the vagaries of very cold weather. Never clip the dog's long hair in winter. That shaggy fur will keep him warm outside, and regular grooming will keep him healthy for maximum protection.

Poisoning: Plants, Pesticides, and Other Toxins

Now there's a real mouthful of trouble. There are dozens of indoor and outdoor plants that can poison your dog. Your Golden's tendency to hunt and explore will lead him to wood piles and weed thickets full of insects, dead animals, and toxic plants. That's his idea of fun!

A single bite of a toxic leaf, stem or flower can cause a wide range of symptoms from simple mouth irritation to vomiting and diarrhea to hallucination, seizures, and death (as with Oleander and Castor Bean). If you suspect plant poisoning, bring your dog to the vet's office immediately. Try to bring a sample of the plant, and if your dog has vomited, bring a sample of that as well.

For complete information on toxic plants, including their scientific names and associated problems or hazards, write to the National Animal Poison Control Center (NAPCC), College of Veterinary Medicine, University of Illinois, Urbana, IL 61801, and enclose a check for $10. The NAPCC Hotline numbers are 1-800-548-2423 and 1-900-680-0000.

Signs of poisoning vary, depending on the substance and quantity ingested. Any one sign or combination requires veterinary attention. Look for:

➤ *Difficulty breathing.* Labored, shallow, or very rapid breathing.

➤ *Unusual behavior.* Pawing at the mouth, holding the mouth open, increased salivation or drooling, frequent swallowing, increased thirst, watering eyes or nose, dilated pupils, or impaired vision.

➤ *Digestive upset.* Diarrhea, vomiting, foul breath, pain when urinating or defecating, tense or tender abdomen, blood in feces or vomit.

➤ *Nervous system.* Shivering, convulsions, uncoordinated movements, coma.

➤ *Cardiac.* Weak or irregular heartbeat.

➤ *Temperature fluctuations.* High or low temperature or swings up or down.

Pesticide Poisoning

Picture this. You walk into the garage and discover that your Golden has just spilled a bottle of plant spray all over the floor and himself, and he might have licked some up. Moments later you discover your Golden cowering under the kitchen table, drooling and shivering, his eyes wild and dilated.

Emergency! Call your vet immediately. If the insecticide is on the dog's fur, shampoo immediately with whatever soap is available. If you know he's eaten or licked some of it, induce vomiting, collect the insecticide, any vomit or residue, grab your Golden, and rush to your vet. Any delay can be costly as the toxins spread quickly through your dog's body.

Doggy Do's

Keep the National Animal Poison Control Center Hotline number near your telephone: 1-800-548-2423. The cost is $30 for as many calls as each case requires. For quick questions without credit card use, call 1-900-680-0000. The cost is $20 for the first five minutes and $2.95 for each additional minute.

According to the NCPC, more animals die each year from insecticide poisoning than from being hit by cars. The National Coalition against the Misuse of Pesticides says that more than 50 percent of all test animals that breathed in fumes from commercial insecticides died. And the EPA tells us that children under the age of 6, animals, elderly people, and people with weak immune systems should not even walk on insecticide treated ground for up to four weeks after application. That should poison your attitude about using pesticides on your lawn!

If you're still not convinced that you should avoid the use of chemicals in your dog's yard and play area, maybe you should live with goldfish instead of golden dogs.

Dances with Skunks

Hopefully your Golden never will, but if he does, this is one job you can handle by yourself. (You probably won't get any volunteer assistance anyway!) The most common odor-removal product is good old-fashioned tomato juice—lots of it. A newer remedy is a mixture of one quart 3 percent hydrogen peroxide, one-quarter cup baking soda, and one teaspoon liquid soap. Some suggest soaking with apple cider vinegar. Whatever you use, the dog's coat must be thoroughly soaked for at least 10 minutes before rinsing. If his eyes have been sprayed, rinse them well before bathing. You might have to repeat the process, and some slight skunk odor might linger for a while. Your efforts will depend on your tolerance level.

Fish Hooks

Fish hooks can lodge anywhere, from the paws to the lip or muzzle. Removal usually requires two people, one to hold the dog and one to use the tools. First cut the barbed end with a tin snip or sharp scissors. Then gently push the remainder of the hook through the skin. Apply an antiseptic to external body parts.

Doggy Don'ts

If your dog has swallowed thread, pantyhose, or something long and stringy, do not attempt to pull it out. You could make things worse. Ditto for the other end. If he is evacuating something long and stringy, let him push it out on his own. If the dog's unsuccessful at either end, rush him to your veterinarian.

Foxtails

These tiny plant parts can be a plague for sporting dogs who spend a lot of time outdoors. The seeds have a barb on one end that catches on the fur. With each movement, the barb will lodge deeper into the hair, then into the skin and genital openings, and can cause painful abscesses that will become infected if not removed immediately. Other prime areas are ear and nasal passages where the foxtail can enter, and then travel through the dog's system causing internal damage and even death. Hunting and outdoor dogs are the most likely victims, but even a brief walk in foxtail country can be dangerous.

Your best weapon is prevention. Keep your Golden out of wheat-type fields, especially in the fall, and brush and examine him thoroughly after every venture into brush or undercover.

Choking

Dogs can swallow anything from chicken bones to balloons. Wrap the dog in a blanket to keep him still. Wedge the dog's mouth open, pull out his tongue, and use your fingers or needle-nosed pliers to remove the object. If it won't come out, lift the dog and hold him upside down by the hind legs. Shake him vigorously to try to dislodge the object and clear his airways. If you're unsuccessful, use the Heimlich maneuver. See your vet for one-on-one instructions.

Muzzling

An injured dog might easily bite the hand that's helping him. A soft muzzle will prevent you from being hurt along with your dog and make your first aid ministrations more effective.

Use a strip of cloth or old hose to make a temporary muzzle, as shown.

Just a Spoonful of Sugar

Yes, even you can give your Golden medication. Read on.

Pill Popping

Do you know how to give your dog a pill without a struggle?

1. Stand behind the dog and grasp his muzzle on each side and tilt his head back.

2. Squeeze gently, pull the top of his muzzle, open and lower his jaw.

3. Place the pill way back on his tongue and poke it toward the side of his throat.

4. Close his mouth and hold it while gently rubing his throat with downward strokes to stimulate swallowing. Tell him to "Swallow."

5. Very important. Always praise lavishly when he swallows the pill.

If the dog refuses to allow you to handle his head or mouth (where did you go wrong when he was a puppy?), use the old hide-it-in-the-cheese trick or bury it in a dollop of peanut butter or liver sausage. (Make sure the pill is compatible with the bribe.)

Doggy Do's

Always check the label on liquid medication to see if it requires refrigeration.

Liquid Medications

To give liquid medicine, use a syringe base minus the needle, an eye dropper, or turkey baster (no glass, please!). Insert the tool into the back of the throat and inject the liquid.

Eye Ointments and Irritations

To apply eye ointment, use your thumb or forefinger to roll back the lower lid gently downward and squeeze the ointment into the exposed pocket. Close the eye and rub *gently*. If you're using a dropper, hold up the upper eyelid and drip the medication inside the top of the eye. Close the lids and rub *very* gently.

You can remove small seeds from under the eyelid using a dampened cotton swab to gently slide the seed onto the swab. Do not attempt to remove other foreign objects. See your veterinarian. Excessive tearing could indicate a blocked tear duct. Again, check with your vet.

Bet You Didn't Know

Periodontal disease is more than just a tooth infection. It puts your dog's kidneys, heart, and liver at risk. How? Bacteria will enter the dog's bloodstream through the damaged gums and travel to his major organs.

Periodontal Disease

Plaque and tartar collect on your dog's teeth just as it does on your own. If it's not removed through brushing or chewing dry dog food and doggie dental toys, it will cause gum disease and tooth loss. Most veterinarians agree that the majority of dogs they treat for dental problems have not received good dental care, and that by age three, 80 percent of dogs exhibit signs of gum disease. Symptoms include yellow and brown build-up of tartar along the gum line, red inflamed gums, and persistent bad breath.

The Spay/Neuter Dilemma

This is really no dilemma. Spay/neuter is more of a no-brainer. First and foremost, a female spayed before her first estrus has a 90 percent less risk of female cancers: cancer of the uterus and/or mammary glands. Males neutered before their male hormones shift into high gear equally reduce their risk of testicular and prostate cancers. Alter your Golden, and your dog is the ultimate winner. Let's examine more good reasons for this important surgery.

Females: Reduced risk of breast cancer, cystic endometrial pyometra, false pregnancies, mastitis which can occur during a false pregnancy, venereal sarcoma, ovarian and uterine tumors, cystic ovaries, chronic endometriosis, vaginal prolapse, uterine torsion, or uterine prolapse.

Your personal benefits: No messy estrus fluids dripping all over your house. No undesirable suitors hanging around the yard.

Males: Reduced risk of testicular cancer, benign prostatic hyperplasia, acute prostatic abscess, tumors around the anus, infection of the testicles, anal hernias, and venereal tumors. He will also hang closer to home and will be much less macho with other male visitors.

Your personal benefits: Absolute birth control for life. Relief from hormone driven urges such as aggression toward other dogs, especially males; territorialism on his home ground; wanderlust to roam around the block; marking with urine at home and in new places; dominance and overt sexual behavior such as riding, sniffing, mounting, licking, and arousal; and your own frustration during his hormonal surges when male dogs resist doing what they're told.

Bet You Didn't Know

Altered dogs are less likely to bite or exhibit temperament problems that would affect your family and neighbors. Surgical alteration will not affect your dog's true personality. He or she will still be the silly, affectionate Golden critter you know and love.

Holistic Veterinary Medicine

Acupuncture, acupressure, homeopathic remedies, natural foods—all are available today to pets as well as people. Many breeders and pet owners who struggle with a constant plague of health and fertility problems have found relief by using natural foods, herbal remedies, and holistic medicine. They use herbal products to treat everything from insect bites, bruises, digestive upset, and whelping problems to fleas and internal parasites, and they claim to do so successfully.

Acupuncture and acupressure are often used on dogs (by licensed practitioners) to treat arthritis and arthritic symptoms, seizures, and other ailments, and even immune problems.

Massage therapy, a relative of acupressure, will strengthen the circulation and flow of energy in your dog, and it's something you can do for free—no vet bill for a change. Geriatric dogs especially benefit from a good massage.

Proponents stress that natural remedies should not replace traditional medical care for serious illnesses, but they definitely have one foot in each medical camp. This is an area of canine care that's worth exploring. Start with a good book on holistic medicine (see Appendix B) and decide for yourself.

The Least You Need to Know

➤ Golden Retrievers are predisposed to skin problems.

➤ Recognize emergency symptoms in your dog.

➤ Know first aid remedies backward and forward, and keep the manual in an easy-to-reach place.

➤ Heatstroke kills. Leave your dog at home on warm days.

➤ Take good care of your dog's teeth, and he will live longer.

➤ Spay/neuter is good for your dog's health and longevity.

That Golden Glow

Grooming your Golden Retriever means more than merely pretty. It's also hygiene and good health. It's all body parts, not just the furry coat. Your own hygiene means more than a shampoo. It's teeth, toes, underarms, and other appendages. Your dog has those same needs, too.

More Than Just a Brush

Grooming does more than untangle and remove dead hair. It also stimulates the oil glands which reduces dander and keeps that Golden fur coat gleaming. It's weekly body checks for lumps and bumps and critters that hide in the skin and coat. It's weekly ear checks and cleaning whenever necessary. It's weekly dental care and monthly pedicures. If all of this sounds like overkill, remember, you're the one who bought this dog!

The Golden Coat

Your Golden's coat is one of its most distinctive features and the one that will require the most care (like once or twice a week) if you want to keep the lid on shedding. The heavy coat actually has two layers: the soft undercoat and the outer guardhairs. Both layers are constantly growing and "dying," a messy process that is enhanced by seasonal weather changes and shifting daylight hours. Without regular attention, the dead hair will stay in the coat and become tangled and matted, and eventually, unmanageable. A well-groomed coat is especially important in cold weather. The flow of air through a dog's coat helps regulate his body temperature, and that process is hampered if the coat is matted or full of mud.

Bet You Didn't Know

Grooming is togetherness. Your attitude toward grooming can make it fun instead of inconvenient. Most Goldens love the hands-on attention involved in grooming, so think of this as bonding rather than a burden. It's one more aspect of living the Golden life.

Use a Brushing Road Map

Brushing will be easier if you follow a pattern on the dog. Always brush with the grain of the coat and start at the rear, working in small sections at a time. Part the coat all the way to the skin as you brush along. Use one hand to hold the hair aside, and then brush from the skin outward through the hair. Work in continuous sections, always brushing upward and forward. Pay special attention to the feathering behind the ears and on the legs and tail as these areas are more prone to matting.

Working the Mats

Remove mats and tangles slowly without yanking so you won't hurt your dog. On larger mats, rub in a few drops of hair conditioner, and then work gently with a mat rake. A slicker brush will handle smaller mats. If you must resort to scissors, cut upward into the mat rather than a straight-across angle cut. While you're brushing, check for rashes, hot spots, and other skin problems.

Tools, Tools, Tools

You'll need more than that slicker brush you bought when your Golden puppy first came home. You'll also need a steel comb with wide and narrow-spaced teeth, a flea comb, and a mat rake. Some Golden owners use a pin brush. I also have a shedding comb, but I end up using my steel comb-slicker brush combination instead. (I also have one of those grooming gloves that collects loose hair when you pet or rub your dog, but I never use it. I just like the feel of my dog's fur between my fingers!) Pick your breeder's or your groomer's brain for good utensil choices.

Doggy Do's

Hint: Use your mat rake or slicker brush to work through mats instead of cutting them out. A straight-across scissors cut will leave an unsightly line in the fur. Even if your Golden is not a show dog, you don't want him to look like a nerd.

Pawdicures

Feet and nails are the most neglected home-groomed areas. I see too many Goldens with paws that look like mops, with long hair spraying from between the toes. Can you picture those feet wet or full of mud?

Hairy feet not only look sloppy, they collect mud, burrs, and ice balls, which is uncomfortable for the dog. Trimmed and tidy feet will also track less mud, snow, and ice into the house. So when you brush and trim his coat, don't forget the feet. Clip the hair around the foot and between the toes and pads, cutting it level with the bottom of the pads.

Nailing Down Nails

Now we're getting personal. There's a confusing variety of nail clippers in the dog foot department. Ask your veterinarian which one he or she recommends and request a demonstration of how to use it properly. It's included in your puppy's visit.

There's great value in 16 well-trimmed nails. It's easier on your furniture and clothing, kids and grandkids. It's also healthier for the dog because nails that are too long can splinter or tear and cause sore feet. Long nails can also cause the toes to splay and spread apart. In the long term, that will damage the structure of the foot, which eventually affects the dog's legs. Now you have a crippled dog. It's amazing what a good pedicure can do.

Trimming Tricks

Nail trimming shouldn't be a wrestling match if you began the process when your dog was a pup. Take your time and be careful not to cut the quick, which is the pink vein visible down the center of the nail. Always cut at a 45-degree angle with the clipper facing the same direction as the toes. If you accidentally cut into the quick, it's no big deal. Just apply a few drops of Kwik-Stop Styptic powder or liquid (or use your own shaving styptic) and allow a few minutes to dry. A bleeding nail is not a tragedy, but it seems to be a nightmare for most dog owners (including me!). If you dread this chore, have your vet or groomer keep your dog's nails trimmed regularly.

Doggy Do's

Handle your Golden's paws frequently during play and petting, and give him a food reward during and after trimming so he associates it with good times, and you won't need your boxing gloves.

Some Goldens have black or very dark nails. If you can't see the quick, hold a flashlight beam directly under the nail to reveal the lighter line of the vein. If you're not sure, make small clips in the tip or curved part of the nail.

Trimming a small amount of nail often is better than trying to cut neglected nails that have grown too long. Walking on cement sidewalks or running and playing in concrete kennel runs helps keep nails ground down. Indoor dogs will need more frequent pedicures.

Clean Teeth = A Healthy Dog

Are your Golden's teeth white and free of tartar build-up? Are his gums pink and firm? Is his breath tolerable, or will it stop an elephant in its tracks? Do you dismiss it as just part of his dogginess? Wrong! Noxious breath is not natural or healthy.

Home dental care is vital to your Golden's long-term health. Plaque and tartar are perfect hosts for bacteria and, if not removed, can cause periodontal disease that is severe and irreversible. It causes serious multiple gum problems and if left untreated, leads to tooth loss and systemic health problems that will affect the liver, kidneys, heart, and lungs. Dry dog foods and plaque-attacker chew products like sterilized hard bones and floss-ropes will help prevent dirt build-up. Keep the chewie bucket full. Include a dental check-up in your annual visit to the vet. Some dog's teeth might need professional cleaning every year.

For a change, you don't need a lot of fancy tools. Cleaning teeth is more elbow grease than gadgetry. You can use a soft-bristled toothbrush and toothpaste made just for dogs. (Toothpaste for people will make your dog sick.) Brush his teeth the same way you would your own, from the gums down with gentle strokes. If he objects, try wrapping a gauze pad around your index finger and rubbing it across his teeth. If your Golden has learned to accept your hand in his mouth since puppyhood (of course he has!), dental maintenance shouldn't be a struggle.

Studies show that 80 percent of dogs show signs of oral disease by age three. Scary, isn't it? Another survey conducted at one veterinarian congress in Vancouver, B.C., determined that dog owners can literally add three to five years to their dogs' lives simply be providing routine dental care. Isn't that reason enough to preserve that Golden grin?

Doggy Do's

If your Golden isn't fond of toothbrushes or gauze pads, try a Finger Brush, which is a toothbrush that fits over your fingers. You can find it in most catalogs and pet stores.

Bet You Didn't Know

You can make your Golden drool over dental sessions by using a poultry-flavored toothpaste made just for pooches. Better yet, it doesn't have to be rinsed out.

Ear Care

Flop-eared dogs, especially water-bound critters like retrievers who love to wallow in ponds and puddles, are more prone to dirty ears and recurrent ear infections than those perk-eared little terriers. The long earflap acts like a terrarium cover that prevents airflow and keeps the ear canal moist and ripe for organism growth.

Recognize the Symptoms

Infected ears usually emit a foul odor and might have a rancid-smelling discharge. The ear canal will be red and inflamed and/or contain debris or a dark, smelly waxy substance. Often the dog will scratch his head—a *lot*—or tilt his head to the affected side.

Take Quick Action

Dog owners make two mistakes with ear infections. They postpone going to the vet until the ear has worsened and the bacteria have multiplied into a more severe infection (what they can't see doesn't appear serious), or they stop treatment too soon, before the infection has been "killed." If treatment starts as soon as possible, you will avoid secondary problems, and the cure is faster and easier on the dog and your pocketbook. Always continue treatment for the prescribed period, or the problem will surely re-occur (canine law of averages).

Attention Means Prevention

Ear problems are easy to prevent. Just pay strict attention to ear hygiene during your weekly grooming sessions. Regular cleansing

218

With their flop ears, Goldens are candidates for ear infections. Regular cleansing is a good preventative.

with a specially formulated ear cleanser, even if the ears don't look dirty, will help loosen any deep-down grime and wax. Drip several drops into each ear and massage it for 30 seconds. Use a cotton ball to absorb excess moisture and a cotton ball or swab to remove any dirt. The cleansers also act as drying agents (important after *every* swimming session) and will correct the pH environment of the ear, which discourages musty growths, particularly in humid climates.

Bathing

This is an area that's often overdone. Most Goldens need a bath every two or three months, although some fastidious owners have their Goldens professionally groomed and bathed every month. The dogs usually don't need it, but it makes their humans happy, and it does help to minimize shedding.

Protect Eyes and Ears

Plug your Golden's ears with cotton balls and keep his eyes dry. Follow the directions for the specific shampoo and be sure to rinse thoroughly. Shampoo residue can irritate the skin. Some owners claim that a warm water rinse will help loosen the dead hair.

219

Anal Sacs

You have to make sure both ends of your Golden are in good working condition. That includes his anal sacs, which are two scent glands under his skin, one on each side of the anal opening. The pockets fill with fecal fluid, and when a dog eliminates, the sacs empty from the pressure of expelled solid matter. Sometimes the fluid collects, and the dog becomes uncomfortable. That's when you see him scooting his rear end across your carpet doing the proverbial choo-choo—always in front of your non-dog guests who will find it absolutely gross.

You should empty these stinky compartments before each bath, or every few months if bathing is less frequent. Anal glands can become swollen and impacted if not emptied, which can lead to infection and surgical correction, so regular tending is important.

The glands are at 4 o'clock and 8 o'clock on either side of the anus. Using your thumb and two fingers of one hand, press inward and upward in those spots to express the fluid contents. Place a paper towel over the opening when you squeeze, or you risk a nasty shot in the eyes. I'm a card-carrying member of the anal sac fluid-in-the-face club, so heed my warning; it's *not* pleasant!

Identification

At the very least, your dog should always wear a collar with an indentification plate and rabies tag attached.

Tattoos and Microchips

Your Golden should have both of these permanent identifications whether he's at home or on vacation. The tattoo is most commonly placed inside the inner thigh. (The ear can be cut off, hardly a pleasant thought, but dog thieves aren't nice people.) Using the dog's AKC number is most commonly recommended because AKC will contact the owner of a lost dog. Because I have several Goldens, I decided to use my social security number and add the first letter of each dog's name to the end 555-55-5555-A. Because two of their names start with "A" I have "A-1" and "A-2." That way I only have one number to register with the National Dog Registry for tattooed dogs (their address is listed in Appendix B) and the AKC Companion Animal recovery Program for tattooed-microchipped dogs.

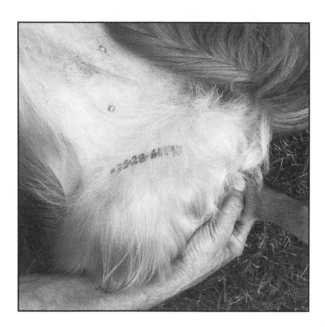

A tattoo on the inside of the dog's thigh is a great permanent identification method.

Don't tattoo your dog when he's very young because the tattoo will grow as he grows and become stretched out and less visible. Anytime after nine months of age is reasonable. Remember to clip the long hair inside that leg frequently to keep the tattoo visible.

A microchip is the newest method of identification and the one most recommended by veterinarians. The microchip is a tiny computer chip about the size of a grain of rice that is implanted under the skin of the dog's neck with a special syringe. The process doesn't hurt, it will not cause any short- or long-term pain or illness, and will remain in that same spot until death.

Doggy Do's

Always keep a spare ID tag on hand in case your Golden's tag is lost and check his collar occasionally to make sure the tag hasn't fallen off.

Let's Get Physical

Exercise will keep your Golden looking great as well as feeling great. In fact, it's as essential to your Golden's overall well being as food and water. It's also important to your own mental health, because a

221

Golden that is not exercised will redirect his energy into creative mischief and destruction. You'll swear Hurricane Andrew came ashore.

If you think dogs will exercise by themselves, you'd better think again. Most dogs, including Goldens, are just like you and me. They move about only if they have a reason to do so. A fenced backyard will not provide physical stimulation for your Golden. *You* are your dog's motivation to run, play, and get physical.

Golden Energizers

Your Golden needs high-energy retrieving games like Frisbee toss and fetch-the-tennis ball. Play on your Golden's natural instincts and throw canvas or plastic bumpers for him to retrieve. If he doesn't bring them back, run in the opposite direction to entice him to chase you. This retrieving business is in his genes; he'll catch on fast. A 15-minute (minimum) backyard retrieving session every day will help keep the average dog in shape.

Doggy Do's

The street salt used on roads and sidewalks during the winter can burn your dog's paws. Be sure to clean his paws after a walk outdoors. It's best to wash, not just wipe, because wiping could actually rub the salt into cracks on and between the toes and do more damage.

Walking for All Ages

Your dog also needs his daily walk. How far and how long depends on the individual dog, so just make sure he can keep up with you without undue stress (on you, too!) and don't push beyond his endurance level. Many dogs don't know what's best for them and will extend themselves beyond their limits. Goldens are notorious for that.

Try to find a park, field, forest preserve, or beach where there are no traffic hazards, and plan a hike or bicycle outing once or twice a week. You don't have to be creative. Just get your dog outdoors for exercise.

Be Weather Wise

On warm days, walk during cooler mornings and evenings, and rest if you notice your Golden is panting excessively. He can become overheated very easily. Hang a water canteen on your belt and stop occasionally for a drink. In extremely cold weather, walk at midday when it's warmer. On summer walks, stay off hot cements or tarred and blacktop surfaces that could burn your Golden's footpads.

Picking Up the Pace

If you're a jogger, your athletic Golden Retriever is a perfect running partner. He not only loves to run, he'll inspire you to stay the course, and you'll both benefit from the emotional bond that will grow from running together.

Before you decide to do the three-minute-mile with your Golden, a quick health check with your vet (for your dog, of course) is a good precaution. Then start out slowly. Out-of-shape dogs will gladly run themselves into exhaustion and then collapse. Make sure your dog can hang in there before you up your speed.

Doggy Do's

If your dog is exposed to extended periods of summer sun during exercise or on long summer walks, protect his nose with a sunscreen formulated especially for dogs. Check your pet supply house or catalog for approved products.

Doggy Don'ts

Never feed your Golden within a few hours of heavy exercise, hunting, or serious training. It could cause cramping, intestinal upset, or a dangerous condition called bloat. Offer food no sooner than three hours before a workout or one hour after. Hunting professionals advise a six-hour food delay before a hunting trip.

Doggy Do's

If your dog licks his feet after running through a field, he could have picked up tiny pointed grass and weed seeds that wedge themselves into the foot tissue. If they're not removed at once, the seeds can become painfully imbedded and infected, which means another trip to your friend, the veterinarian. Always check the feet after an outdoor jaunt.

Do a Critter Check

Examine your dog for ticks and other foreigners after each outing in the summer. Brush his coat to clear out weedy debris and check his toes and underarms.

Whatever your exercise pleasure, keep your Golden on a leash! There are dozens of doggie temptations that could turn your morning mile into a nightmare chase scene. Even the most reliable dog can defy his owner and zip off after a squirrel, often across a busy street. A leashed dog is seldom a statistic.

The Least You Need to Know

➤ Grooming is important to your Golden's health.

➤ Grooming includes your dog's coat, feet, nails, ears, and teeth.

➤ Good dental hygiene will add healthy years to your dog's life.

➤ Exercise is a must to keep your Golden looking good and feeling good.

➤ Do a complete dog check after dog walks.

Chapter 20

Hereditary Diseases

In This Chapter

➤ Eye disease

➤ Epilepsy

➤ Hip dysplasia

➤ Elbow disease

➤ Hypothyroidism

➤ Subvalvular Aortic Stenosis

➤ von Willebrand's disease

Pull up a chair. Unfortunately, our very popular Golden Retriever comes complete with several serious hereditary problems that either shorten his lifespan or make life difficult or painful.

The most common and most well known is, of course, hip dysplasia. Despite many years of X-ray screening before breeding, hip problems in the breed have not reduced significantly.

Less widely known but just as serious are cataracts and heart disease, elbow disorders, epilepsy, and thyroid malfunction that causes a pot-pourri of health problems. Add allergies to the mix, and you just want to cry if you love the breed as much as I do. I'll try to keep this simple and discuss these problems in alphabetical order.

Eye Disease

Several inherited eye disorders affect those big, brown Golden eyes.

Cataracts

A cataract is defined as an opacity of the eye lens, and several types are common in the Golden breed. At least one hereditary type shows up early in life. Some cataracts don't interfere with the dog's vision, while others progress into partial or complete blindness. Cataract surgery is successful in some cases, but it's expensive.

Retinal Dysplasia

Retinal dysplasia (RD) is an inherited defect of the retinal lining that is not uncommon in Goldens. Unlike Progressive Retinal Atrophy, it does not result in complete blindness, but it can render a hunting dog worthless in the field or for other working tasks. RD-affected Goldens should be eliminated as candidates for breeding.

A few hereditary, but less serious, eyelid and eyelash problems also affect the breed. The bluish haze often seen in the eyes of older dogs is a normal aging process and is not hereditary or a breeding problem.

Only a board certified ophthalmologist can determine if a dog is free of eye disease. Eyes should be examined annually until eight years of age because certain forms of cataracts can develop throughout the dog's life. Dogs who have been properly examined will be issued an ophthalmologist certificate. Clearances can then be registered with the Canine Eye Registry Foundation (CERF). All breeding stock should have eye clearances, and the breeder should produce an ophthalmologist's proof of clearance or a CERF registration certificate.

Epilepsy

Epilepsy is a seizure disorder caused by abnormal electrical patterns in the brain. It can be hereditary or caused by a variety of environmental factors, including viral and infectious diseases, trauma, or chemical and nutritional imbalance. Inherited epilepsy usually appears between six months and three years of age, and some experts believe that epilepsy that occurs in later years might be genetically induced as well. Recurring seizures can be controlled with medication, but long-term medication sometimes causes other health problems. The disease itself doesn't affect a dog's health or longevity. Although hereditary epilepsy is difficult to diagnose, dogs that suffer recurring seizures should not be bred, and experts familiar with the breed also recommend against breeding parents and siblings of those dogs.

Hip Dysplasia (HD)

Simply stated, hip dysplasia means poor development of the hip joint. It's an inherited disease that's complicated by environmental factors such as over-nutrition, rapid growth, and excessive trauma during developmental stages. The condition covers a broad range of severity that includes mild, moderate, and severe levels of dysplasia. A severe case can render a working dog incapable of performance. Even a mild case can cause painful arthritis in a sedentary companion animal, although some dysplastic dogs live normal, active lives.

The only currently accepted diagnosis is through X-ray. X-rays are evaluated by the Orthopedic Foundation for Animals (OFA), and dogs with "clean" hips are issued an OFA number that includes a rating of Excellent, Good, or Fair. OFA certifications issued after the mid-1990s will also appear on the dog's AKC registration papers. Dogs must be at least two years old before their joints are eligible for OFA clearance.

PennHip evaluation is a second method of hip examination that was developed at the University of Pennsylvania School of Veterinary Medicine. This method also uses X-rays but examines other hip qualities such as joint laxity and can be used to evaluate dogs as young as 16 weeks of age. Although relatively new, PennHip gains greater acceptance every year, and some breeders now use both methods to screen their dogs.

At this time, only OFA-approved dogs should be used for breeding. A pedigree with more than one generation of OFA is still the best insurance a Golden puppy buyer has for obtaining a Golden who won't be plagued with hip problems early or later in life. Reliable breeders always screen their breeding animals and will proudly produce those OFA clearances on their dogs.

Make sure that your puppy's parents have been cleared of all hereditary maladies before you bring your pup home.

Elbow Dysplasia (ED) and Osteochondritis Dissecans (OCD)

Both of these diseases are developmental irregularities of the bone and cartilage, and are a major cause of front end lameness in many large breed dogs. Both ED and OCD affect young dogs, with typical symptoms of recurring or intermittent lameness usually appearing between four and seven months of age. Radiographs (X-rays) taken of the elbow joints and shoulder will verify the condition.

In 1990, OFA created an elbow registry to provide a database for dogs who have been X-rayed and certified free of ED and OCD. Although both diseases are believed to be hereditary, nutrition is also thought to be a contributing factor in their development. Feeding diets high in calories, calcium, and protein are suspect, and at least two major dog food manufacturers now offer puppy growth foods that are low in fat and calories and recommended for fast-growing large breed dogs. Please read the next chapter on nutrition for details on properly feeding your Golden puppy.

As with hip dysplasia, Goldens with ED or OCD should not be bred.

Hypothyroidism

Hypothyroidism is a complex disease characterized by the malfunction of the thyroid gland. Symptoms include obesity, lethargy, recurrent infections, skin or coat problems such as hair loss, dryness, and thinning fur. Treatment consists of daily oral thyroid supplementation that could continue for the dog's entire life.

Testing is rather tricky and should be handled by a veterinarian familiar with thyroid problems and this breed. Dogs who are diagnosed with hypothyroidism should be re-tested annually to continue therapeutic levels of the hormone. Most breed experts agree that dogs with hypothyroidism should not be used for breeding.

Subvalvular Aortic Stenosis (SAS)

This disease is as bad as it sounds. A dog with SAS can simply drop over dead without any other symptoms or a moment's warning. The disease involves a stricture in the left ventricle of the heart that restricts the blood flow out of the heart, leading to sudden and unexpected death after normal activity or exercise.

As a hereditary disease, there appears to be greater incidence of SAS in certain lines or families of Golden Retrievers. Goldens as young as 8 to 16 weeks of age can be examined for SAS, although they should be re-evaluated at 12 to 24 months before they are considered as breeding candidates. Certification requires examination by a board certified veterinary cardiologist.

von Willebrand's Disease (vWD)

vWD is the most common hereditary bleeding disorder in canines, wherein puppies inherit a lack of clotting ability from their parents. On certain tragic occasions, it isn't diagnosed until the dog is spayed or neutered and bleeds uncontrollably during surgery. von Willebrand's is sometimes also linked with hypothyroidism, creating a double whammy for those poor affected animals.

The Least You Need to Know

➤ The Golden Retriever breed is affected by several serious hereditary diseases.

➤ A Golden with an inheritable disease should never be bred.

➤ Be sure your puppy's parents have all their clearances.

➤ Every Golden owner should have a complete understanding of Golden hereditary problems.

Chapter 21

Nutrition: The Great Dog Food Debate

In This Chapter

➤ Quality food equals good health

➤ Pondering proteins

➤ The real skinny on high fat

➤ Feeding the growing pup

➤ Counting calories for senior dogs

Feeding your Golden is like putting gas in your car. You can't use watered down fuel and expect good maintenance or peak performance. Likewise, you can't feed your dog sub-standard dog food and expect to have a healthy active animal who will live to a ripe old age. So what's a captive consumer to do? Get smart. Know the proper way to fill your Golden's nutritional gas tank.

If you remember one thing about dog food, it should be this. If you want to save money on dog food, don't spend less. Cheaper is not economical in the long run. It costs less to use a premium dog food than an economy brand because of the nutritional power packed in the better food. Countless studies have proven that you have to feed as much as five times the amount of cheap food to get the same nutritional benefits of the premium foods. Additionally, your dog could end up with dermatitis-skin problems from a lack of the vitamins and minerals he needs to support healthy skin and coat. Even if the food bag doesn't say "generic" on the label, if it's an off-beat brand—beware.

Protein Power

Why is protein the big gun in your dog's food bowl? Because about 50 percent of the dry matter in a dog's body is made up of protein, which is an essential component of its cell structure. The absence of quality protein can result in poor growth, weight loss, poor hair coat, impaired immune function, depressed appetite, energy loss, irregular estrus, poor reproductive performance—among other things! We serve our dogs "higher protein" and "all-meat protein" and hope we're dishing out a better meal.

Protein requirements change throughout a dog's life just as it does in ours. The animal's size and age, his individual energy demands, and daily stressors vary from dog to dog. Optimum protein intake is more crucial at certain times in most dogs' lives. During pregnancy, a bitch needs 26 to 28 percent protein to help the fetuses grow and develop properly. Growing puppies need at least 26 percent protein to help ensure proper bone and tooth development during periods of heavy growth.

Doggy Do's

Although animal fat is a real yummy for dogs (bacon grease, meat fat), vegetable fat is better for his skin and coat. A dog with a dull coat or flaky skin might benefit from a tablespoon of safflower or canola oil added to his food. More is not better. Feeding larger amounts can make him fat.

At one time, the high levels of protein in growth foods were thought to contribute to structural problems such as hip dysplasia and other skeletal disorders like OCD. Current research holds that calories, primarily from fat, not protein intake, are the likely culprit.

Large breeds such as Golden Retrievers just naturally grow fast, which puts a big strain on young and fragile joints. A high-fat puppy diet promotes rapid growth and weight gain, thus increasing the risk of hip and elbow dysplasia and other skeletal problems. While the

Dogs need fat for a healthy, shiny coat. Vegetable fat, derived from safflower or canola oil, is best for your Golden.

average dog owner might think you need to feed, feed, and feed to keep that growing body growing, research has shown that over-feeding actually contributes to poor joint development.

At least two major dog food manufacturers have developed growth foods for the various breed sizes with a lower fat content to meet a large-breed puppy's restricted caloric needs. The object is to keep the puppy lean during his major growth phase of three to eight months.

The Real Skinny on High Fat

Fat calories have their place, however. Dogs need fat for healthy skin and coats and to prevent constipation. An adult dog food should contain 10 to 15 percent fat to keep a healthy animal healthy. Although animal fats are more palatable, fats derived from vegetable oils are a better source of the fatty acids dogs need to lubricate their outsides.

Fat also contains more than twice the metabolizable energy of protein, so a Golden who hunts or works at other strenuous activities will need extra fat, not protein, to maintain his energy and stamina. Watch for terms like "calorie-dense" or "high caloric density" in performance food because they refer to the fat content of the food.

Preservatives

Dog foods require preservatives because they contain fats that will spoil when exposed to heat and air (called oxidation). Manufacturers use antioxidant materials to prevent that process. The antioxidants used might extend the fat life, but some add dangers worse than rancidity to the food. One preservative frequently used is called ethoxyquin, which is a recognized cancer-causing agent, as are two others known as BHA and BHT. The preservative used will be listed on the label and might be shown on the front of the bag as well. Many dog foods today are preserved safely with vitamin E, or you can purchase natural foods with no preservatives from specialized dealers. Ask your veterinarian about those products if they interest you.

Vitamins and Minerals

Briefly stated, don't add vitamins and minerals to your dog's food. A quality dog food (the key word being *quality*) should be complete with no supplements necessary to meet the life stages of the pet. In fact, supplementation can create toxicity problems, causing poor growth, abnormal eye conditions, and impaired reproductive performance.

Supplementation is especially dangerous for puppies. If extra calcium, phosphorous, or vitamin D is added to a puppy's diet, it can cause skeletal disorders.

If you had one dog food rule to follow, it should be no vitamin supplements. If you feed your Golden a complete and balanced diet made by a reputable manufacturer, he's getting all the nutrients he needs. I have a couple of favorites (but if I share them with you here, the others would complain), and all I add is love!

Senior Dog Food

Here's another protein myth: high protein diets cause kidney disease in older dogs. Not so. Although an already damaged kidney cannot properly metabolize protein, the protein itself will not cause the problem.

That said, most dog food manufacturers do offer a somewhat lower protein food (ideally 15 to 20 percent) for senior canines (just in case)—in large breeds defined as dogs over seven years old. Because the amount of protein is restricted, the quality of the protein becomes vitally important. Healthy older dogs still require adequate quality protein to maintain lean body mass and help support their immune system.

Food Allergies and Hypoallergenic Diets

Because allergies top the Golden list of health problems, diet can have a major impact on your dog's overall well-being—and *your* mental health as well! Natural foods and hypoallergenic diets use less common protein sources such as lamb, turkey, or fish that are less irritating to the dog. Some highly allergic dogs do well on homemade diets. Homemade might help your dog, but it's also lots of work and requires a firm commitment from the owner to follow a strict dietary regimen. See Appendix B for books on feeding your dog holistically.

Bet You Didn't Know

You can make your Golden's meal more palatable by sprinkling a dash of garlic powder on his food. It's good for him, too!

If your dog has food allergies, work with your vet or a canine nutrition specialist (find one through your veterinarian, kennel club, or a veterinary teaching institution) to develop a diet he can tolerate.

Digestibility

How do you know if your dog is getting the full benefit from the food he eats? Good digestibility should produce two to three firm and normal stools each day. I check my dog's stools often to make sure everything that comes out is A-OK.

Wet or Dry Food

Should you add water to dry food? That's optional. A dog that gulps his food like it's his last meal could inhale the dry particles or choke on them and might do better with a generous splash of water in his food. It's also thought that adding water helps reduce the risk of bloat. I add about a half to one cup of water to each dog food pan immediately before offering it. The food is still crunchy enough to preserve dental benefits, and I think the water releases flavor and adds to palatability (although eating ravenously has never been my dogs' problem!). Always have fresh water available for your dog at all times, even if you add water to his food.

Hold the Anchovies

Dog owners love to gooey up their dog's food. It's another way of lavishing attention. Bad idea. It usually makes the dogs fat and possibly unhealthy. Table scraps are no big deal if given in moderation (as in not-much-not-often!). A bit of fruit, vegetable, or potato won't hurt most dogs occasionally. Although it adds extra calories, it shouldn't upset the nutritional balance of a good commercial diet.

Feeding table scraps carries another subtle danger: the finicky eater. If a dog gets used to goodies in his food bowl, he might refuse to eat his normal diet. The best treat is still not to treat, or give his veggie treat separate from his dinnertime.

Obesity

"Obesity shortens a dog's life quite considerably, a life which is much too short anyhow." Konrad Lorenz (1903–1989), Austrian psychologist and animal behaviorist.

Studies indicate that obesity is the number-one nutritional disorder in dogs and that a large percentage of pet dogs seen by veterinarians in this country are overweight. An extra 10 pounds on your should-be-65-pound Golden would be comparable to an extra 20 pounds on a woman who should weigh 120.

Keep Your Dog Slim

Just like people, every Golden is an individual with different metabolic needs. The same "food × exercise" ratio that keeps one dog lean and physically fit might lead to obesity in another. You have to know your Golden. Your dog should have an hourglass figure when viewed from above, with a defined waistline behind his rib cage and in front of his hind legs. Put your hands on his back with your fingers curled around his rib cage. You should be able to feel his ribs easily with very slight pressure. Does your vet hint (or bluntly state) that your Golden is too fat? I see too many Goldens who are overweight, and their vets fail to discuss it with the owner. Some vets might fear losing or antagonizing a client who might not like to hear the truth.

Doggy Don'ts

No chocolate for your Golden. Pure chocolate is toxic in doses that are proportionate to the dog's weight. About 2½ ounces of unsweetened chocolate can be fatal for a 25-pound dog, and a two-pound bag of chocolate chips could kill a 50-pound dog. Hide those chocolate goodies!

Bet You Didn't Know

Onions are highly toxic to dogs. The vegetable contains an alkaloid that ruptures the red blood cells, causing fever, darkened urine, and death! Cooking does not eliminate the danger, so skip the fried onions on your pooch's meat tray, please.

Obesity is simply excess consumption—too many calories in and too few calories used—and is no healthier in dogs than it is in humans. It can lead to diabetes and skin problems and will aggravate orthopedic problems, heart conditions, and nervous disorders. It *will* shorten your Golden's life. Either cut back on food portions and/or the type of food and increase his exercise. Doing both is better.

The Least You Need to Know

➤ Always feed your Golden a quality name-brand dog food.

➤ Learn how to read the label on a dog food bag.

➤ Feed a dog food appropriate for your dog's age and activity level.

➤ Do not add supplements or table scraps to your dog's food.

➤ Onions and chocolate could poison your dog.

Part 5

Living the Golden Life

Get ready for the time of your life! Golden Retrievers are the most versatile breed on four paws. Whatever your doggie dreams or pleasure, this breed can take you there. The multi-talented Golden is the most accomplished of all the retriever breeds and excels in every canine competition or activity. They also wear more helper's hats than any of their canine counterparts, serving as guide and assistance dogs, drug detectors, and gentle therapists. Yet despite their grand accomplishments, they're still happiest as home companions, retrieving sticks in the back yard, and sharing your popcorn, curled up beside your easy chair. What more could you ask of any dog?

Getting through your first Golden year is a major step toward living a Golden life together. But as with all things doggy, there's always so much more to learn. Signs of old age and how to care for your dog when he gets up in years are important things to know about.

This part of the book covers that vast array of Golden opportunities you can share with your Golden and how to make his later years happy and healthy.

Chapter 22

The Do-It-All Golden Retriever

In This Chapter

➤ Water and retrieving

➤ Gold medal accomplishments

➤ Golden social workers

➤ Your Golden's full potential

➤ Goldens serve society

➤ Get to know the GRCA

Despite the Golden Retriever's amazing ability to excel at almost every activity devised for dogs, about 95 percent of all Goldens serve as all-American bed warmers and family companions. Nevertheless, you should still know what's in your Golden's genetic bag of tricks. You'll be amazed and inspired at the vastness of this breed's accomplishments. And who knows? Maybe you'll be inspired to dip your dog's paws into something more exciting than daily walks, tennis balls, and TV talk shows.

Swimming

No doubt about it, Golden Retrievers love the water: lakes, ponds, puddles, and the muddier the better. If you're into swimming and wet dogs, you've chosen the right breed. Swimming comes naturally to Golden puppies, although some might take a little longer to get beyond the puppy-paddle stage.

When introducing your Golden puppy (or Golden of any age) to water for the first time, observe the Golden (water) Rule. Never force or throw your puppy or dog into the water. Your Golden must go in the water on his own. You can lure, entice, cajole, and beg, but never ever force.

A Pleasant First Swim

A Golden's introduction to water should always be a positive experience. Start with a beach or pond with a shallow shoreline, warm water, and a warm day. Some Golden puppies take one look at water and dive in head first without a second thought. Most will puppy-paddle at first, but a few will take off swimming like a porpoise.

Put on your aqua shoes and wade in with your puppy. Toss a toy and use lots of encouraging praise. Start in running water up to his elbows or belly, and as he shows confidence, toss the toy a little farther each time. If he gets nervous or refuses, back off and stay in shallow water for a while. Never scold or force. Use your three *P*s again: Praise, Patience, and Practice!

Retrieving

Tennis ball, Frisbee, retrieving bumper, fallen branches—if your Golden is like mine, he will retrieve them all—and retrieve—and retrieve until he drops! This dog knows that retriever is the better half of his name! Whether you plan a serious retrieving future for your Golden or just hope to have a little fun, the right start in retrieving basics will help you both enjoy this natural ability.

Start with a Soft Bumper

With a seven- or eight-week-old puppy, begin with a soft puppy bumper made from an old white sock (because white is highly visible) stuffed with more old socks. A soft paint roller is another good choice. Use your "bumper" for retrieving only, never for play time or any other purpose. If you have a pigeon wing, fasten it to the sock with tape.

Goldens just love getting wet!

Start Indoors

This is kind of an extension of the puppy-toy-retrieving games. A good place to begin is indoors in a long hallway. Close any doors so there's no escape route and your pup has nowhere to run except back to you. Be sure the bumper is conspicuous on the flooring surface.

Rev Up the Motor

Flash the bumper under the pup's nose to get him excited, and then toss it just a few feet in front of him. Throw straight ahead at his eye level, sort of a skimmer throw, because an eight- or nine-week-old puppy has very limited range of vision and can't follow objects that move rapidly up, down, or sideways. Use your "Fetch" command and lots of praise when he retrieves. Encourage his return and praise him once again *while he still has the bumper in his mouth*. (If you take the bumper immediately, he will associate coming back with your taking the bumper away and will learn not to come back.) Now remove it gently with more praise and toss again.

Do Three Retrieves and Stop

Start with three short, easy retrieves a day in the same lesson, *never* more, and less if your dog's enthusiasm fades. Always stop when he's

243

still eager to retrieve again. The biggest mistake most people make is offering too many retrieves until the pup or dog gets bored and tired of the game.

Move the Game Outside

Once the dog gets the idea, move your lessons outdoors on short-cut grass and start with two or three retrieves of 20 or 30 yards, less if he can't follow where you toss it. Increase the distance gradually as your dog succeeds.

At some point during this scenario, the dog's going to take off with that bumper and head for the far corner of the yard. ("This is *my* bumper!") No problem. Attach your 30-foot-long line to his collar. The moment he picks up his bumper, call him with a "Come" command and give a gentle tug to remind him to return. (Don't reel the dog in like a fish. If he still resists, use a series of gentle tugs, only at those moments when he's back pedaling or stops moving toward you.) Run backward as you're calling him excitedly to entice him back to you. (Remember those "chase" games from Chapter 11?) Most retriever puppy owners quickly learn to act wild and crazy to keep their puppies motivated!

Add a "Gunner"

Once your puppy is returning without too much resistance, you can add a thrower or "gunner" to his lessons. As with all dog lessons, when you add any new element to a lesson, back up a step (in this case, shorten the distance of the throw). Still working on mowed grass, the gunner stands 20 or 30 yards away while you hold your pup. The gunner calls "Hup, hup" while you tell your pup to "Mark." Once the pup's attention is focused on the gunner, nod your head to signal for the throw with more "Hups." (No huge throws for little pups.) Release the puppy while the bumper is in mid-air and don't forget to act wild and foolish again on his return. If he has trouble finding the bumper or going the entire distance, shorten the throws until he is successful. Success is the main ingredient in his basic training.

Train with Experienced People

Beyond this point, if you want to pursue field work with your Golden, you'll need a good book or two on training retriever puppies for hunting. If your Golden puppy's a retrieve-a-holic, scour gun dog books and magazines and join a retriever club or hunting club (it doesn't have to be just Goldens) to find an experienced training partner.

Gold Medal Performers

For the Golden Retriever owner with a competitive streak, there's a world of dog activities to explore. Conformation (dog shows for show dogs), obedience trials (shows for obedience-trained dogs), hunting tests, field trials, tracking tests, agility trials, working certificate tests—these Golden Retrievers can do it *all* and do it *well*! (Of course, I'm prejudiced; but you already knew that!)

Conformation

If conformation sounds a little stuffy, let's just switch to "showing dogs." Dog shows are basically beauty contests, the Miss and Mr. America of dogs. The winners earn points that apply toward the future title of show champion, which appears as a Ch. before his name on his pedigree. Show Goldens are judged on the physical properties listed in the breed standard in Chapter 2.

Grooming and Gaiting Your Golden

"Showing your dog" means more than just trotting around the breed ring with your handsome Golden. Proper grooming is an art and one that could affect a judge's opinion of your dog. "Gaiting," the way your Golden walks and runs, is another aspect of showing you both need to master.

Find an Experienced Golden Owner

Most importantly, you need an experienced person to evaluate your dog and help you get started. If you purchased your puppy from a show breeder, work with the breeder to decide if your pup has show potential. Try to find a Golden Retriever club in your area or join a local kennel club where you'll meet other people who show their own breeds in conformation. Attend some dog shows and talk to Golden Retriever exhibitors. Perhaps your veterinarian can direct you to a breeder or a club so you can meet other dog show fanciers. If your beloved Golden has no show potential, love him for all his other fine qualities and consider purchasing your next Golden from a reliable breeder with a good track record who will be willing to help you get started.

Obedience Competition

Obedience is another "ring" activity, only this time looks don't count. Your Golden will have to master several basic obedience routines (stuff you already learned in puppy class!) and achieve qualifying scores (a minimum of 170 out of a possible 200 points) in three different obedience shows to earn a title that will appear on his pedigree. It's that simple. And it's fun!

Bet You Didn't Know

Every year, more Golden Retrievers become obedience trial champions (OTCh) than any other breed.

Obedience Titles and Prizes, Too

Obedience titles are earned on three levels of competition, with each level presenting a greater degree of difficulty. In the Novice class, the dog earns a CD (Companion Dog) title. In the Open class, your dog earns a CDX (Companion Dog Excellent). The Utility class offers a UD (Utility Dog) title. A dog has to come up through the ranks and earn his obedience titles from the bottom up. Each class also offers placement awards of first through fourth place, so if your Golden performs his exercises to near perfection, he can earn a trophy, too.

Although some Golden puppies are "natural" game retrievers, all hunting dogs need to be trained.

Join a Dog Training Club

If you'd like to dabble in obedience, find a training club or check with a local kennel club for classes in advanced obedience. The American Kennel Club will send you their booklet *Rules and Regulations for Obedience Competition* if you write to them at the address shown in Appendix B. You should also invest in a book or two devoted to obedience training. There are literally dozens on the market, and several are listed in Appendix B.

Hunting: Events and Challenges

Now we're into feathers and retrieving birds. Is your Golden out of hunting stock? Does he go bonkers to retrieve even non-bird objects? If you'd like to fulfill the heritage envisioned by Lord Tweedmouth, you have lots of choices.

Hunting

Is your outdoor passion waterfowl or upland game? If your Golden is from hearty hunting stock, that Golden nose will lead you to unspeakable pleasures in the field. Of course, you'll have to deal with a muddy dog, cockleburs, and other field debris in his Golden coat, but a game bag stuffed with birds is worth it.

Like all performance athletes, a good hunting dog needs fine tuning before he knocks your socks off in the field. You should team up with other hunters or field trainers when your Golden is still young to build good retrieving habits early in the game. A well-trained hunting retriever will be the envy of your hunting buddies, but *well-trained* is the key phrase here. If this is your first hunting experience or your first working retriever, find a professional trainer or people involved in the sport to learn the basic principles of field training that your dog will need to become a good hunting partner. Beg, borrow, or buy a few books on training a retriever for the field. See Appendix B for suggestions.

Hunting Tests

Hunting tests are designed for the non-competitive sportsman who may or may not actually hunt but wants to work with his retriever in the field. Hunting tests consist of three levels designed to test a retriever's natural abilities with graduated levels of difficulty. The tests are pass-fail, and each dog is judged against a standard of performance and does not have to outwork another dog to qualify.

Launched in 1985, AKC retriever hunting tests have grown into a major event in the world of sporting dogs. Retriever owners and their dogs (real-life hunting dogs as well as retrievers who just love birds, water, and retrieving) work with freshly shot game birds (ducks and pheasants) under simulated hunting conditions to prove their dogs' natural hunting ability. Dogs that complete the requirements as set forth in the AKC rules for hunting tests receive a corresponding title that will appear after the dog's name on his pedigree. Write to AKC for *Regulations and Guidelines for AKC Hunting Tests for Retrievers*.

Wait! There's more. The United Kennel Club (UKC) and the North American Hunting Retriever Association (NAHRA) also offer a non-competitive hunting test program complete with game birds, gun safety provisions, and titles for the dog. Both organizations are listed in Appendix B.

Field Trials

This is the granddaddy of sporting retriever events and dates back to 1931. Licensed by the AKC, field trials are a big step up from hunting tests and showcase the superstars of the working retriever world. Competition is ferocious, and only the best survive to capture the wins, placements, and points required to earn the title of Field Champion (FC) or Amateur Field Champion (AFC). Field championships are the most prized of working titles, particularly because this is an all-breed sport with Labradors, Goldens, and Chesapeakes competing on the same playing field.

Field trials differ from hunting tests because dogs are eliminated on the basis of their performance when compared to that of other competing dogs. Dogs are tested on both land and in water under more rigid circumstances than in hunting tests. The tests are designed on four ascending levels of difficulty to challenge both younger and more experienced dogs. The vast majority of the dogs entered have some degree of professional training, so a novice owner-handler is at a huge disadvantage. I hate to sound discouraging, but this is an expensive and highly competitive sport that requires enormous dedication to training and a thick hide to endure inevitable failures. With 50 to 100 dogs competing in most stakes and only four placements awarded, it's no wonder this is often called a loser's game. If you decide to try it, start with the best caliber Golden you can afford, purchased from a reliable breeder with field trial experience (as proven by the accomplishments of the breeder and the parents of the pups).

For the AKC *Field Trial Rules and Standard Procedure* manual, write directly to AKC at the address listed in Appendix B. As with hunting tests and hunting, training books and videos abound, and you'll be smarter and more successful if you read a few.

Working Certificate Tests

Finally, a field event devoted just to Golden Retrievers. Working certificate tests are very basic, non-competitive field tests sponsored by the Golden Retriever Club of America to encourage and evaluate the instincts and natural abilities of Goldens in the field. The dogs are tested on both land and water against a set standard of performance, and they are not expected to perform anywhere near the level of the field trial or hunting test retriever.

Designed with two levels of difficulty, the WC (Working Certificate) requires a short (35 to 50 yards) double retrieve on land and two shorter single retrieves in the water. The WCX (Working Certificate Excellent) consists of a longer triple retrieve on land, a double retrieve in water, with added difficulty to demonstrate trainability in the dog. The tests are sponsored by GRCA member clubs across the country and are open to all AKC-registered Goldens. Most clubs hold practice training sessions before the tests to offer assistance to newcomers and club members.

Complete rules and regulations are available from the GRCA secretary (listed in Appendix B) or from any area Golden Retriever Club.

Doggy Do's

If your Golden is a retrieve-a-holic or if he loves to hunt a little or a lot, Working Certificate tests provide excellent forums where you and your Golden can show off and have a grand time doing what your dog loves best. So get out there and have some fun!

Tracking: Making Dog Scents

Tracking is actually a distant relative of obedience trials, only the dog works independently and follows his nose to prove his scenting ability. The dog must follow a track, a path walked by a stranger, across complex terrain that includes twists and turns, fences, hedgerows, and other hazards. Two AKC titles are offered, and the tests are sponsored by AKC-licensed dog clubs. To earn a TD (Tracking Dog) title, the dog must complete a 400 to 500 yard track. The TDX (Tracking Dog Excellent) faces a more complex track of 800 to 1,000 yards. Tracking buffs hail this sport as exciting and exhilarating for themselves as well as their dogs! Complete rules are available in the *Tracking Regulations* from the AKC.

Agility

Is your Golden a Frisbee fanatic? Does he climb the kids' slide at the park? Can he leap tall buildings in a single bound, or at least jump on his doghouse? Then he might be a natural for agility. In agility events, the dogs race through a complex course of obstacles to jump over, crawl under or into, cross over, straddle or weave through. They are judged on speed and accuracy, earning both qualifying scores and placements for their performance. The sport is open to all breeds of dogs, but our athletic Goldens usually excel. Agility enthusiasts have a favorite saying, "Try it, you'll like it!"

Agility clubs are turning up in most major cities, so if you're interested, check with your veterinarian, a local kennel club, or write to the national agility organization listed in Appendix B. *The Rules and Regulations for Agility Trials* are also available through AKC.

Goldens Serve Society

Take a healthy dose of all those Golden Retriever activities mentioned earlier, add the Golden's great willingness to please, and you have the ultimate public servant—and he'll never dip his paws into campaign funds!

Assistance Dogs

As skilled assistance dogs for the physically disabled, Golden Retrievers pull wheel chairs, pick up books and pencils, turn on lights, open refrigerator doors, and complete dozens of other daily tasks for their handicapped person. Goldens easily master complex tasks and minute details, and are especially adept at sensing their owner's needs and wishes. Assistance dog owners state emphatically that their dog has made the difference between merely existing and living a quality life.

Guide Dogs for the Blind

Golden Retrievers, Labrador Retrievers, and German Shepherds are the three breeds most widely used as guide dogs for the blind. A guide dog's primary responsibility is what the name implies: to guide the owner in public in heavy crowds, public transportation, traffic, and other busy areas. Guide dogs are raised the same way as assistance dogs—by volunteer puppy-raisers until they are 12 to 18 months of age, when they enter formal training. Dogs who complete the program are matched to the physical and mental characteristics of the blind recipient. A list of the five U.S. guide dog training schools is included in Appendix B.

Hearing Dogs

Hearing dogs are canine alarm systems for their deaf owners. A Golden Retriever hearing dog will alert his owner to as many as a dozen different sounds: a door bell, an alarm clock, telephone or smoke alarm, a baby's cry, a window surreptitiously opened by an intruder. Companion Goldens can easily be trained for this task if their owner suddenly becomes deaf. Some assistance dog providers also train hearing dogs or can refer you to an organization that does.

Drug Dogs

From airports to seaports to land border ports, Golden Retriever drug detection dogs patrol their drug beats in search of illegal narcotics and other contraband substances. Thanks to their superior scenting ability, they can sniff out everything from marijuana and cocaine to cash and alcohol. If there's a down side to a Golden's service in the drug force, it's his huggability and happy personality, which might present a non-threatening figure to the criminal. Nevertheless, dozens of Golden supersleuths work for the U.S. Customs Service and other law enforcement agencies as part of the nation's growing army of drug detection dogs.

Arson Dogs

Arson detection dogs are trained to sniff out gasoline, kerosene, and other types of accelerants that can be used to start a fire. In this area of law enforcement, even modern science has difficulty competing with the Golden nose. Arson officials have recorded cases of canines locating a fire site under inches of ice and water and in places where lab technology failed to find accelerants. Fortunately for us, a Golden just thinks he's having fun sniffing around a fire scene.

Search and Rescue Goldens

You've seen them on TV, dogs searching through rubble after an earthquake or a bombing, looking for survivors buried under concrete and debris. Known as Search and Rescue (SAR) dogs, they work for no reward other than the pleasure of the work itself, finding a human being. SAR Goldens also assist local law enforcement agencies searching for children and people who are lost or victims of suspected crimes.

For more information on canine search and rescue operations, contact the National Association of Search and Rescue (NASAR) at P.O. Box 3709, Fairfax, VA 22038.

Therapists in Golden Armor

Too bad we can't invent a Golden Retriever pill. The breed is arguably more therapeutic for the physically and emotionally disturbed than any medication in the marketplace. Take two brown eyes, soft silky fur, a wildly wagging tail, and a dog that senses what you need at any given moment in a crisis, stir well, and pet, and you have a Golden Retriever Doctor Feelgood.

Goldens are active in nursing homes, hospitals, children's wards, prisons, and schools. They work with all ages and all human conditions, and make each and every one feel better about themselves or their predicament. As Roy Rogers used to say, "Happy *tails* to you. . . ."

Golden Retriever Club of America

The Golden Retriever Club of America (GRCA) is the national umbrella organization formed in 1938 to direct and protect the future of the breed. In those days, Golden fanciers recognized that a breed with so many varied talents could be exploited by breeders who specialized in specific disciplines. Unfortunately, they were right.

The GRCA today is still dedicated to the preservation and advancement of the breed as a superior hunting companion. With over 5,000 members, it is one of the largest breed clubs in the world. Its officers, directors, and dozens of national committees oversee a multitude of breed activities and research projects that benefit not only Golden Retrievers, but the general dog population as well. Over 50 member clubs in more than two dozen states offer Golden guidance and camaraderie to people who own and compete with or just plain enjoy their Goldens. Every year these clubs host dozens of specialty shows, hunting tests, and field events, and educational seminars and clinics across the country to encourage owners to train and work with their Goldens and join the fun.

For more information on the GRCA, contact a local Golden Retriever club or the American Kennel Club, 260 Madison Ave., New York, NY 10016.

The Least You Need to Know

➤ A Golden's favorite activity is retrieving and retrieving.

➤ Goldens love the water; take your Golden swimming.

➤ Goldens excel in almost every doggy sport.

➤ Find an experienced person if you want to try a dog sport.

➤ Golden Retrievers make excellent service dogs.

➤ Golden owners should know about and support the GRCA.

Chapter 23

Golden Oldies

In This Chapter

➤ Recognize signs of aging

➤ Geriatric check-ups

➤ Adopting older Goldens

➤ Rescue Goldens

➤ Letting go

Large breeds like Golden Retrievers mark the beginning of their geriatric period at about eight years of age. Your Golden might still look and act like a puppy, but don't be fooled. He's entering his sunset years.

Of course you want to make his golden years as healthy as your own, and being a smart dog owner, you know that senior dogs need special care. Besides his check-up once a year, what else can you do to prolong his life and keep him healthy longer? For starters, rigid weight control and proper oral hygiene are the two primary canine life extenders.

Weight

Obesity strains every major system of a canine's body and *will* take years off your dog's life. As your Golden ages, his energy needs will decrease, so you should adjust his food portions accordingly as well as the type of food he eats. Overweight dogs need a high-fiber, low-fat diet. Dogs over seven or eight years old should eat a "senior" diet designed for aging dogs (read the bag!). If you're changing diets, consult your veterinarian first.

Teeth and Gums

Just as important as his weight, good dental hygiene will add healthy years to your dog's life. Too many dogs die early because of heart, kidney, liver, or respiratory infection and disease, conditions that started at the gum line and could have been prevented with good dental hygiene.

Bet You Didn't Know

Your Golden's gums should be a healthy pink, with some pigmentation if that's what he was born with. His teeth should be white, although some slight yellowing is normal with age. Very pale or whitish gums are warning signs that say "Take me to the veterinarian!" They are symptoms of a circulation problem that can be due to any number of serious and life-threatening conditions.

Periodontal disease is caused by plaque and tartar build-up. Dry dog food, hard dog biscuits, and hard chew bones help reduce tartar, but nothing replaces good old-fashioned tooth brushing. Many experts recommend brushing every day, but weekly is a minimum and probably a more reachable goal. Start when your dog's just a pup, and he'll learn to accept and enjoy the process. Ask your veterinarian to demonstrate the proper method. If you don't brush, have the dog's teeth professionally cleaned twice a year. Studies show that 85 percent of dogs over 6 years of age have some form of periodontal disease, which is an infection in the deep portions of the gums. If it's not treated promptly, the infection enters the bloodstream and can become life threatening in an older dog with an equally old immune system. The infection will attack his vital organs, resulting in heart, respiratory, kidney, or liver disease.

Exercise and Arthritis

Exercise is important at every life stage, but it should be tailored to fit your dog's age and physical condition. A senior dog who is sedentary for long periods will grow out of shape more quickly and will take longer bouncing back.

Walking and running are still the best maintenance workouts. Even the change of scenery will stimulate him mentally, and he'll be extra grateful for the time you spend together. Be careful not to overdo it. Some Goldens have more heart than stamina and will press on even when exhausted. (Sound like someone you know and love?) If he seems to tire quickly or appears to be hurting the next day, slow down and see your vet.

If your dog has arthritis, make sure he has a soft, warm place to rest and sleep. If your Golden doesn't already have one (he should!), surprise him with one of the many cushy orthopedic dog beds, and put it in his favorite place and out of drafts. I guarantee he'll sleep like a baby—I mean, a puppy. My old Golden has several beds all over the house so she can be comfy whenever she's with me. For some unspoken reason, my other Goldens never even try to sleep on one of her beds. You should know that arthritic conditions are significantly more prevalent in obese dogs. Watch that diet!

Vision

If you notice a change in your senior Golden's eyes or vision, it could be due to cataracts, genetic disease, or simply old age. In many cases, a veterinary ophthalmologist can surgically remove the cataracts and dramatically improve his vision.

Many geriatric dogs develop lenticular sclerosis, a hardening of the lens that causes a bluish-gray haze or tint in the eyes. It does not affect vision or require treatment. However, whenever you notice any change in your dog's eyes, see your veterinarian to determine the problem and how treatable it is.

Hearing

Some dogs grow deaf with age; others never do. Try to distinguish between "selective hearing" when he just wants to ignore you, and actual hearing loss. When my 13-year-old Golden stopped hearing the treat jar open, I knew she wasn't faking it. Like most hearing-impaired dogs, she startles easily, so I avoid sudden movements and gently stomp the floor before I touch or pet her so she doesn't jump. We've developed a communication system of hand signals to say "Time to come in," "Let's go," "I mean right now!" and other conversational gimmicks.

Beware of hearing loss in a "city" dog. He won't hear a car approaching on the street or in the driveway. I personally know of dogs that have been killed because of their deafness.

Lumps and Bumps

Some lumps are normal; many are not. While grooming or just petting your Golden, feel his entire body for lumps and bumps. Although skin masses like cysts, warts, and fatty tumors are common in older dogs, you should always have your vet inspect any new growths you find. Cancer in all breeds of dogs has become more common and can attack any organ or body part. Breast and testicular cancers are common in unspayed bitches and intact males. Early spay/neuter is the best prevention.

Coat Condition

A little gray hair here and there is normal, but overly flaky skin and hair loss can indicate a late onset hormonal problem with the thyroid gland. (A dog's thyroid gland gets tired and wears out just like its human counterpart.) Your vet can diagnose hyperthyroidism and treat it with an oral replacement dose of supplemental hormones.

Heart Disease

How do you know if and when it happens? Changes in sleeping habits, restlessness, coughing (especially at night or on first waking in the morning), panting, shortness of breath, and decreased exercise tolerance can indicate cardiovascular problems. If you catch the problem early, you will have greater success in treating it.

Older Goldens tend to get gray hair (just like humans). But dry skin and hair loss are signs of a hormonal problem, easily treated by your veterinarian.

Kidney Disease

Does your dog urinate more frequently? Does he now have accidents in the house or have to urinate in the middle of the night? Does he drink more water than he used to? All are symptoms of kidney or bladder disease or diabetes.

Unfortunately, by the time you see any of these symptoms, there is *already* significant and irreversible damage to the heart or kidney. His kidneys will be over 50 percent damaged before those signs show up. And if you miss the signs of increased thirst or urination, the dog continues to get worse.

The prevention key in all of these old age diseases is to know your dog and be observant.

Incontinence

Urinary incontinence is a common problem in older spayed bitches. They start to unconsciously dribble urine. You might be surprised to find wet spots on her bed in the morning. This is one condition that is easily remedied with a supplemental hormone that can improve the muscle tone of the bladder.

Dogs over seven years of age should have annual blood and urine analysis to test for kidney and liver function before those visible signs appear. Dogs who are already in kidney failure can be managed with special diets prescribed by the veterinarian to reduce the workload on the kidneys.

Babies and Older Goldens

Just as important as introducing puppies to children, you need to make sure your adult golden accepts your new baby with loving paws. Up until now he was the center of your universe, and now he has to share that turf with something small and squirming. You have to convince him this infant is not a threat and will not diminish the quality of his life. Before you have your new little one, prepare your Golden so he won't feel threatened and will view this newcomer as his new best friend.

Obedience Review

It's a good idea to review your Golden's obedience training so he's sharp on his commands. A dog that sits and stays is much easier to control when you have to change a diaper. Obedience training will also make your Golden feel important again and less intimidated by a new arrival.

Doggy Don'ts

A word of caution: Never leave your dog alone with your new baby. A baby's cry can sound like prey—just like a rabbit's scream. Don't take any chances.

Play Dates with Kids

If your dog has never been exposed to toddlers, introduce him to children away from your home and invite them later to visit you at home. Go to parks and playgrounds so your dog can interact with lots of kids.

Keep Life Normal

Try to keep your dog's schedule as normal as possible during the adjustment stage. He will be more content and therefore more cooperative. If he shows resentment, fear, or other negative reactions, be patient and encouraging, but do consult your veterinarian. If such behavior continues, you should seek help from a qualified professional to help your dog adjust.

Adopting an Older Golden

If the thought of struggling through housetraining and canine puberty appalls you, consider the joys of adopting an older Golden Retriever. When you adopt a dog that has grown through the cute, bouncy puppy stage, what you see is what you get.

You don't have to guess about the coat type, adult size, or the personality in a dog who has outgrown puppyhood. An older or more mature Golden might even be housebroken and have some degree of basic house manners or training. Of course, puppies are great fun, but they're also a lot work, often very frustrating work, and you can spare yourself that struggle if you bypass adolescence and go directly to adulthood.

If you worry that an older Golden will not bond or relate to you because you didn't nurture him from infancy, forget it. An almost unfortunate fact about this breed is that they will love just about anyone who loves them back. As much as I hate to think about it, I know that my beloved Goldens would be just as happy with someone else who loved and cared for them the way I do. That's just the nature of this sweet beast.

Adult Golden Sources

You can sometimes find adult Goldens and older Golden puppies through a breeder, Golden Retriever rescue services, or animal shelters.

Breeders

On occasion, a breeder takes back a puppy or older Golden from a previous litter for some unfortunate reason (something legitimate like divorce or allergies, and some inexcusable: he barked too much, jumped on the kids, got hair in the pool, didn't have time, and so on). The breeder will evaluate the dog before placing him in another home to prevent another life change for the dog. If you work with a breeder, make your preferences known so she can arrange a perfect match. Review the early chapters on puppy goals and selection and apply those same criteria.

Rescue Groups

Golden Retriever rescue services work with animal shelters, animal control agencies, and dog owners to assist in relocating and rehabilitating abandoned, abused, and confiscated (from puppy mills and brokers) Goldens into healthy, loving homes. There are at least 35 rescue services affiliated with Golden Retriever clubs across the country that rescue and re-home thousands of Goldens every year.

If you work with Golden Rescue to find an older puppy or adult (puppies come along infrequently), you can usually rely on their evaluation of the dog, their choice for you, and their help in his adjustment to his new environment. The last thing they want is for this dog to be uprooted once again. Expect them to be firm and possibly intimidating to make sure you're the right person for this dog. They already know the dog. They *don't* know you!

Animal Shelters

Many animal shelters work with area breed rescue groups when a purebred dog arrives. If there is no Golden Retriever organization or dedicated volunteer to assist with the adoption, the dog goes into the general shelter population. Shelters in smaller communities of under 100,000 often work with a few reliable individuals who raise certain breeds and are willing to assist or act as an adoption agent on their own. The vast majority of shelters have the dog's best interests at heart and do their best to screen and evaluate their animals to determine if they are adoptable and to assure a good match with the adoptive person.

When you visit a shelter, bring a prepared checklist from Chapter 6 (even though these are adult dogs). Don't be shy. Ask lots of questions and spend time alone with the dog before you agree to take him home. Your best choice is that middle-of-the-road guy we always talk about. Not too timid or too pushy, and never aggressive in any way. Don't cave in or feel sorry for a dog that isn't right for you or who could present more problems than you're prepared to handle. The awful truth is you and I can't save them all.

There will be paperwork with each adoption agency, whether shelter or rescue organization, which is for the dog's protection as well as yours. They will charge an adoption fee that might include certain health services for the dog. All require that every adopted Golden must be spayed or neutered.

If you adopt or purchase an adult Golden or older puppy, bring him home during a vacation period or at least over a weekend when you can spend two or three days helping him adjust to his new home. Use the same procedures outlined in Chapter 6. All dogs, regardless of age, need reassurance and attention to make them feel safe and comfortable in a new environment.

After a reasonable adjustment period, take your new Golden to obedience school. Like all Goldens, he'll love doing something with his person, he'll enjoy learning new things, and he'll especially like knowing you're in charge, which is the main benefit of the obedience experience.

Letting Go

Living the good life with a Golden also means the inevitable: we will probably outlive our dogs. Despite our best efforts to keep our dogs young and healthy, the time comes when we have to say goodbye. If your Golden friend suffers from cancer or other terminal disease, he will look to you, his caretaker and best friend, for relief from constant pain or inability to function. After 30 years of living with this magical breed, I've faced that moment many times. Each time it's a brand new decision, never easier, and always filled with the same gut-wrenching pain. Euthanasia is the most difficult decision of dog ownership and possibly the most unselfish. Your dog deserves your help when it's time for him to go.

When It Is Time

You'll know. Please believe me, you will know when that moment comes. I learned that again just recently during the writing of this book. One of my older Goldens fell ill, and I knew it would soon be time. But as I heard the bad news in the emergency clinic on a Sunday morning, I didn't have that deep gut feeling that I needed to be sure. We had three more grand days together, he and I. He was comfortable and very loved and spoiled. He left with grace and dignity and died peacefully in his sleep, sparing me, for once, that dreadful final trip. Fortunately, this time, waiting was the right decision.

Your veterinarian will help you make your decision. Five years ago when my senior female Golden was stricken with a tumor and suffered an exceptionally bad day, my vet assured me it was not yet time and pleaded with me to believe her, that my heart would tell me when. She was right, and a week later, I knew that moment had arrived. I treasure those last days we had together.

Stay with Your Dog

Most owners elect, as I do, to remain with their dogs to hold and comfort them during their last moments. It's best to stay as calm as possible, but I believe in my own heart that my dog understands why he's there and needs to hear me say "I love you" one more time. The veterinarian will inject a drug that takes but a second to make the dog drowsy, fall asleep, and then his heart will simply stop. If you are unwilling or unable to be with your dog, be sure a family member or a friend that he loves stays with him. As difficult as this is, your Golden buddy does not deserve to die alone.

As I write this chapter, my oldest Golden lies beside my chair. At 13½ she's still in apparent good health, but every day I remember that today is one more gift.

Grieving

Grief is very personal and individual. Some people can't even talk about losing their dog without breaking down completely. Many will cry and grieve for weeks and months before they can remember the happy times without a tear. That's normal and okay. Your dog's death is a huge personal loss, and you should let your emotions show. There will be those few who claim "It's just a dog" and won't understand why you continue to be upset. Non-pet people just don't get it. Be patient with them but don't let other people tell you how to grieve. Share your grief with other dog lovers who have traveled this lonely road. It's going to take time. All those memories will eventually bring smiles instead of tears.

Getting Another Golden

Should you get another dog? Some people don't want to endure another heartbreak and vow never to get another dog. Some of those will change their minds. Others want a new dog right away. Most of my friends own two or more dogs not only because they love living with a bunch of dogs, but because they won't be without a dog when one dies. I could not deal with losing one of my dear friends if I didn't have a Golden army here to comfort me. But that does not diminish the unique "specialness" of the dog I lose. It just represents my personal consolation zone.

Whether you get a new dog right away or wait until your heart has healed, approach your new dog as a special individual and don't compare him to your last one. None are the same, and each one is your best friend.

Burial

My husband and I have our dogs cremated. For years we buried our Goldens in one of their favorite places, up on a hill on our farm under a grove of trees where we walk our dogs each day. Today cremation is available, and we bury their ashes with their Golden brothers and sisters on that hill. Friends might question my sanity, but I always wave a big hello whenever we walk past their spot. I believe they're watching over me.

You might choose to bury your dog or his ashes in your yard or under a tree or bush in some favorite place. You can keep the ashes in a sealed vase or urn on your desk or mantle, or scatter them in your yard or over a pond where he loved to swim. Pet cemeteries offer plots and headstones. Whatever your choice, your Golden will live on in your heart forever.

The Least You Need to Know

➤ Senior Goldens require special care and annual vet visits.

➤ Keep your older Golden slim and keep his teeth clean.

➤ Old age problems can be avoided if you watch for signs.

➤ Older Goldens make great family companions.

➤ Rescue groups are good sources of adoptable Goldens.

➤ Your vet will help you know when it's time to let your Golden go.

Glossary of Titles and Abbreviations

AKC Conformation Titles

Ch.   Bench (Show) Champion

Dual Ch.   Conformation and Field Champion

AKC Obedience Titles

CD   Companion Dog

CDX   Companion Dog Excellent

UD   Utility Dog

UDX   Utility Dog Excellent

OTCh   Obedience Trial Champion

AKC Tracking Titles

TD   Tracking Dog

TDX   Tracking Dog Excellent

VST   Variable Surface Tracking Dog

UDT   Utility Dog Tracking

UDTX   Utility Dog Tracking Excellent

AKC Field Titles

FC   Field Champion

AFC   Amateur Field Champion

FC-AFC   FC and AFC

JH   Junior Hunter

SH   Senior Hunter

MH   Master Hunter

AKC Agility Titles

NA   Novice Agility

OA   Open Agility

AX   Agility Excellent

MX   Master Agility

United States Dog Agility Association (USDAA) Titles

AD   Agility Dog

AAD   Advanced Agility Dog

MAD   Master Agility Dog

JM   Jumpers Master Dog

SM   Snooker Master Dog

RM   Relay Master Dog

VAD   Veteran Agility Dog

ADCh   Agility Dog Champion

Golden Retriever Club of America (GRCA) Titles

WC   Working Certificate

WCX   Working Certificate Excellent

OS   Outstanding Sire

OD   Outstanding Dam

SDHF   Show Dog Hall of Fame

OBHF   Obedience Dog Hall of Fame

FDHF   Field Dog Hall of Fame

VC   Versatility Certificate

VCX   Versatility Certificate Excellent

***   Qualified all-age status, earned with a first or second place in Qualifying or a JAM (Judges award of merit) in an Open or placement in an Amateur

**   Placement or JAM in a licensed Derby stake

*   Has earned a Working Certificate

United Kennel Club Titles

U-Ch   Bench (Show) Champion

U-CD   Companion Dog

U-CDX   Companion Dog Excellent

U-UD   Utility Dog

HR   Hunting Retriever

HR-Ch   Hunting Retriever Champion

GRHR-Ch   Grand Hunting Retriever Champion

U-AGI   Agility One (Novice)

U-AGII   Agility Two (Advanced)

U-AGIII   Agility Three

U-AGCh   Agility Champion

North American Hunting Retriever Association Titles

SR   Started Retriever

WR   Working Retriever

MHR   Master Hunting Retriever

GMHR   Grand Master Hunting Retriever

Canadian Kennel Club Titles

OTCh   (AKC Utility Dog)

FTCh   Field Trial Champion

AFTCh   Amateur Field Trial champion

WC   Working Certificate

WCI   Working Certificate Intermediate

WCX   Working Certificate Excellent

ADC   Agility Dog of Canada

AADC   Advanced Agility Dog of Canada

MADC   Master Agility Dog of Canada

Miscellaneous Titles

CGC   Canine Good Citizen

TD   Therapy Dog

TDI   Therapy Dog International

Common Canine Terminology

ADOA   American Dog Owners Association

AKC   American Kennel Club

Alpha   The top (or boss) dog in a pack

Blind   A field term meaning a bird that is planted in a hidden location on land or water

CKC   Canadian Kennel Club

CERF   Central Eye Registry Foundation

CGC   Canine Good Citizen, an AKC title

Dam   A canine's female parent

ED   Elbow Dysplasia

GRCA   Golden Retriever Club of America

HD   Hip Dysplasia

ILP   Indefinite Listing Privilege (See Appendix C)

Mark   A bird that a dog sees fall after it is shot or thrown (a field term)

NAHRA   North American Hunting Retriever Association

OCD   Osteo Chondritis Dessicans (elbow disease)

OFA   Orthopedic Foundation for Animals

Pedigree   Canine family tree of ancestors

RD   Retinal dysplasia (eye disease)

SAS   Subvalvular Aortic Stenosis (heart disease)

Sire   A canine's male parent

USDAA   United States Dog Agility Association

UKC   United Kennel Club

vWD   von Willebrand's Disease

271

Recommended Reading and Resources

The Golden Retriever Breed

Bauer, Nona Kilgore. *The World of the Golden Retriever; a Dog for all Seasons.* Neptune City, NJ: TFH Publications, 1993.

Bauer, Nona Kilgore. *The Proper Care of Golden Retrievers.* Neptune City, NJ: TFH Publications, 1997.

Cairns, Julie. *The Golden Retriever: All That Glitters.* New York: Howell Book House, 1998.

Fischer, Gertrude. *The New Complete Golden Retriever.* Second Ed., New York: Howell Book House, 1994.

Foss, Valerie. *Golden Retrievers Today.* New York: Howell Book House, 1994.

Golden Retriever Club of America. *Introduction to the Golden Retriever: GRCA.* c/o American Kennel Club, 260 Madison Ave., New York, NY: 10016.

Schler, Marcia. *The New Golden Retriever.* New York: Howell Book House, 1996.

Behavior and Training

Benjamin, Carol. *Mother Knows Best: The Natural Way to Train Your Dog.* New York: Howell Book House, 1987.

Boyer, Steve. *K-9 Counter-conditioning.* 1321 Long Meadow Dr., Glenview, IL 60025. (Video).

Dunbar, Ian. Ph.D., MRCVS. *Dog Behavior: An Owner's Guide to a Happy Healthy Pet*. New York: Howell Book House, 1999.

Dunbar, Ian. Ph.D., MRCVS. *Sirius Puppy Training*. Oakland, CA: James and Kenneth Publishers, (Video).

Evans, Job Michael. *The Evans Guide for Civilized City Canines*. New York: Howell Book House, 1990.

Fogle, Bruce, DVM, MRCVS. *The Dog's Mind*. New York: Howell Book House, 1990.

Kilcommons, Brian. *Good Owners, Great Dogs*. New York: TimeWarner Books, 1992.

McLennan, Bardi. *Dogs and Kids: A Guide for Parents*. New York: Howell Book House, 1993.

The Monks of New Skete. *How to Be Your Dog's Best Friend*. Boston: Little Brown, 1978.

Pryor, Karen. *Don't Shoot the Dog! The New Art of Teaching And Training*. New York: Bantam Books, 1984.

Rutherford, Clarice, and David Neil. *How to Raise a Puppy You Can Live With*. 2nd Ed., Loveland, CO: Alpine Publications, 1992.

Vollmer, Peter. *Super Puppy*. P.O. Box 3539, Escondido, CA 92025.

Volhard, Jack, and Wendy Volhard. *The Complete Idiot's Guide to a Well-Trained Dog*. New York: Howell Book House, 1999.

Field Training

Quinn, Tom. *The Working Retriever*. New York: E.P. Dutton, Inc., 1983.

Rutherford, Clarice, and David Neil. *Retriever Puppy Training*. Loveland, CO: Alpine Publications, 1986

Spencer, James. *Retriever Training Tests*. 2nd Ed., Loveland, CO: Alpine Publications, 1997.

Walters, Ann and D.L. Walters. *Training Retrievers to Handle.* Olathe, KS: Interstate Book Manufacturers, 1979.

Walters, Ann and D.L. Walters. *Charles Morgan on Retrievers.* Stonington, CT: October House, Inc., 1974.

Love 'Em, Hunt 'Em, Test 'Em—Hunting Tests for Retrievers. AKC, 260 Madison Ave., New York, NY 10016. (Video)

Obedience, Agility, Tracking

Bauman, Diane. *Beyond Basic Dog Training.* New York: Howell Book House, 1986.

Johnson, Glen. *Tracking Dog, Theory and Methods.* Westmoreland, NY: Arner Publications, 1975.

Simmons-Moake, Jane, *Agility Training: The Fun Sport for All Dogs.* New York: Howell Book House, 1991.

Health

Carlson, D.G., DVM, and James Griffin, MD. *Dog Owner's Home Veterinary Manual.* New York: Howell Book House, 1994.

Pet Emergency First Aid: Dogs. Apogee Communications Group, 159 Alpine Way, Boulder, CO, 80304. (Video).

Pitcairn, Richard, DVM, and Susan Hubble Pitcairn. *Dr. Pitcairn's Complete Guide to Natural Health for Dogs and Cats.* Emmaus, PA: Rodale Press, 1982.

Schoen, Allen, DVM, and Pam Proctor. *Love, Miracles and Animal Healing.* New York: Simon & Schuster, 1996.

Schwartz, Cheryl, DVM. *Four Paws, Five Directions, a Guide to Chinese Medicine for Cats and Dogs.* Berkeley, CA: Celestial Arts, 1996.

Volhard, Wendy and Kirby Brown, DVM. *The Holistic Guide for a Healthy Dog,* New York: Howell Book House, 1997.

Dog Organizations

American Dog Owners Association
1920 Route 9
Castleton, NY 12033

American Kennel Club
260 Madison Avenue
New York, NY 10016
212-696-8200

American Society for the Prevention of Cruelty to Animals
441 E. 92nd St.
New York, NY 10128

Bird Dog Foundation
505 West Highway 57
P.O. Box 774
Grand Junction, TN 38039

Canadian Kennel Club
89 Skyway Ave.
Etobicoke, Ontario M9W604R

Delta Society
P.O. Box 1080
Renton, WA 98057-1080

Ducks Unlimited
One Waterfowl Way
Memphis, TN 38120
1-800-453-8257

Humane Society of the United States
2100 L Street NW
Washington, DC 20037

Master National Retriever Club
58 Sweetland Ct.
Lake Jackson, TX 77566
409-297-99443

National Amateur Retriever Club
and the National Retriever Club
4379 S. Howell Ave.
Milwaukee, WI 53207
414-482-2760

National Association of Search and Rescue (NASAR)
P.O. Box 3709
Fairfax, VA 22038

North American Hunting Retriever Association
P.O. Box 1590
Stafford, VA 22555
540-221-4911

Therapy Dogs International
6 Hilltop Rd.
Mendham, NJ 07945
201-543-0888

United Kennel Club
Hunting Retriever Club Inc.
100 E. Kilgore Rd.
Kalamazoo, MI 49001
616-343-9020

Assistance Dog Organizations

Canine Companions for Independence
P.O. Box 446
Santa Rosa, CA 95402

Freedom Service Dogs, Inc.
980 Everett St.
Lakewood, CO 80215

Helping Paws of Minnesota, Inc.
P.O. Box 12532
New Brighton, MN 55122

Paws with a Cause
1235 100th St. SE
Bryon Center, MI 49315

Support Dogs of St. Louis
10755 Indian Head Industrial Blvd.
St. Louis, MO 63132

Guide Dog Schools

Guide Dog Foundation for the Blind, Inc.
371 E. Jericho Turnpike
Smithtown, NY 11787

Guide Dogs for the Blind, Inc.
P.O. Box 1200
San Rafael, CA 94915

Guide Dogs of the Desert, Inc.
P.O. Box 1692
Palm Springs, CA 92263

Leader Dogs for the Blind
1039 Rochester Rd.
Rochester, MI 48063

Pilot Dogs, Inc.
625 West Town St.
Columbus, OH 43215

How to Register Your Golden Retriever

By registering your dog with the AKC, you receive a certificate that records your dog's owner, sire, and dam.

AKC Registration

To register a dog with the American Kennel Club, you must first complete the registration form received from the breeder. Fill in the dog's name in the designated boxes that stipulate 25 letters or less. Write in your name as the new owner. If two people are to jointly own the dog, record them on one line as "Mary and John." If one person is to be the primary owner and the other the co-owner, enter those names on the lines designated for owner and co-owner. Sign and send to AKC at 260 Madison Ave., New York, NY 10016 with the stipulated registration fee.

Confirmation usually takes from four to six weeks. Call the AKC if you have questions.

AKC Indefinite Listing Privilege (ILP)

AKC offers an ILP number for dogs who are purebred but have no proof of parentage. ILP registered dogs can be shown in AKC licensed performance events but are not eligible to be shown in conformation. To obtain an ILP number, the owner must send good quality photographs of the dog, frontal view and both sides, along with a spay-neuter certificate from a veterinarian. Contact the AKC for more details on how to present the necessary information.

Index

291